SPAS AND SPRINGS IN WALES

SPAS AND SPRINGS IN WALES

Audrey Doughty

ISBN: 0-86381-728-9

Cover design: Sian Parri

First published in 2001 by
Gwasg Carreg Gwalch, 12 Iard yr Orsaf, Llanrwst, Wales LL26 0EH
✆ 01492 642031 ▤ 01492 641502
✆ books@carreg-gwalch.co.uk   Internet: www.carreg-gwalch.co.uk

'To Melanie'

CONTENTS

OLD COUNTIES

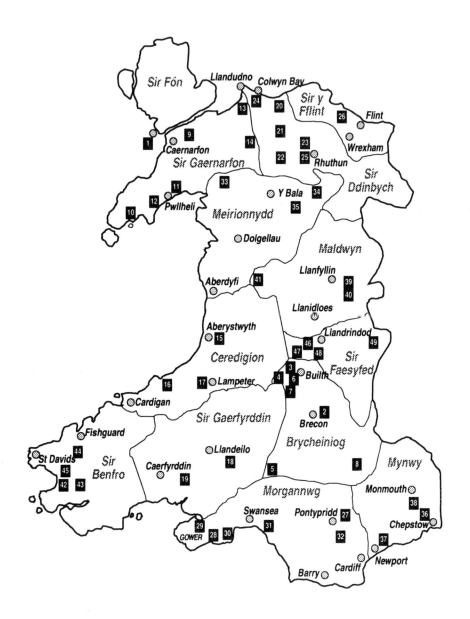

MAP REFERENCES

No.

Anglesey (Sir Fôn)
1. Ynys Llanddwyn – Ffynnon Dwynwen

Brecknockshire (Brycheiniog)
2. Brecon (Aberhonddu) – Priory Well and Penginger Well
3. Builth Wells (Llanfair-ym-Muallt)
4. Cilmeri – Ffynnon Llywelyn
5. Ystalyfera – Ffynnon Cwm-twrch
6. Llangammarch Wells
7. Llanwrtyd Wells
8. Parishow – Ffynnon Isho

Caernarfonshire (Sir Gaernarfon)
9. Llanddeiniolen – Ffynnon Cegin Arthur
10. Aberdaron, Llŷn – Ffynnon Fair, Uwchmynydd
11. Llangybi, Llŷn – Ffynnon Gybi
12. Mynytho, Llŷn – Ffynnon Fyw
13. Llandudno – Haulfre Gardens Well
14. Trefriw Spa

Ceredigion (Cardiganshire)
15. Aberystwyth
16. Llanarth – Ffynnon Gloch
17. Llangybi – Ffynnon Gybi

Carmarthenshire (Sir Gaerfyrddin)
18. Carreg Cennen Castle Well and Llwyndewi
19. Llanarthne – Middleton Hall

Denbigh (Sir Ddinbych)
20. Bodrhyddan Hall – Ffynnon Fair
21. Cefn Meiriadog – Ffynnon Fair
22. Derwen – Ffynnon Sara
23. Llandegla – Ffynnon Degla
24. Llanelian-yn-Rhos – Ffynnon Eilian
25. Llanrhaeadr-yng-Nghinmeirch – Ffynnon Ddyfnog

Flintshire (Sir y Fflint)
26. Holywell – Ffynnon Wenfrewi (St Winifred's Well)

Glamorganshire (Morgannwg)
27. Pen-rhys – Ffynnon Pen-rhys/Ffynnon Fair

Swansea and Gower (Abertawe a Gŵyr)
28. Caswell – St Peters
29. Llanrhidian
30. Oxwich
31. Swansea – St Helen's Well
32. Taff's Well – Ffynnon Daf/Ffynnon Dwym

Meirionnydd
33. Blaenau Ffestiniog – Ffynnon Fihangel
34. Corwen – Ffynnon Sulien
35. Llandrillo – Ffynnon Drillo

Monmouthshire (Mynwy)
36. Chepstow Wells
37. Maindee – Ffynnon Efa
38. Trelech – The Virtuous Wells

Montgomeryshire (Maldwyn)
39. Llanfyllin – Ffynnon Fyllin/Ffynnon Coed y Llan
40. Meifod – Ffynnon y Clawdd Llesg
41. Penegoes – Ffynnon Gadfarch

Pembrokeshire (Sir Benfro)
42. St David's and St Non's
43. St Justinians
44. Llanllawer – Ffynnon Llanllawer
45. Trefin

Radnorshire (Sir Faesyfed)
46. Llanbadarn Fynydd – Ffynnon Dewi
47. Llandegly – Blaen Edw Wells
48. Llandrindod Wells
49. Pilleth – Ffynnon Fair

INTRODUCTION

Wales is often referred to as the Land of Song, but one cannot help wondering whether it should not also be called the Land of Springs. Old maps are peppered with the word *ffynnon* (well) and many still exist, though all are not easy to find.

Some springs have dried up altogether. Wells have been built over, and others seem simply to have disappeared – perhaps destroyed during the Reformation. Some are not traceable because their names have been changed, or original locations are no longer identifiable where something has caused the water to be diverted.

Very many were Holy wells – some having healing properties and fascinating rituals from the past attached to them. Others were secular and purely for medicinal purposes – the springs often being chalybeate or saline and containing sulphur and barium, although the latter was rare. They often had eye wells nearby.

Throughout the country, there are springs of pure and of enriched water – some just popping up in people's gardens. Others have been channelled into a town's water supply and some; Llanrhidian on the Gower in south Wales, Brecon in mid Wales and Trefriw in the north, to name but three – are bottled and sold.

The Romans, when they finally managed to occupy Wales, must have been delighted. Although they left no legacy of grand bath houses (that task tended to be carried out in the 19th century), there is reference in nearly every Welsh spa's history to Romans having used the springs.

Sadly, these days, none of the spas are really fully operative like those found on the continent, but some are still open and have visitor centres that offer at least the experience of bygone days and, in the cases of Trefriw and Llandrindod, an opportunity to drink the water.

To write about every well would be repetitive, result in several volumes, and not make very interesting general reading – except perhaps for the specialist in the field who already has material enough. The country has been divided into geographical areas to facilitate visitors to explore those that still exist. The boundaries of the present Welsh counties are too wide, and it therefore seemed more practical – and perhaps more fitting for wells that have been there for centuries – to use the old boundaries. It is, however, indicated in the index in which of the new counties these wells are now situated.

RITUAL AT HOLY WELLS

' . . . what we call 'superstition' in the modern Welshman is, in reality, a survival of the religious convictions of his earlier ancestors. The pagan gods did not die: they were not allowed to.' Francis Jones (2)

Not all so called 'holy wells' were necessarily situated near churches or chapels. Some could be found by mounds or by megaliths. Mainly of pagan origin, these would have been later appropriated as places of Christian usage. While this could mean that a new place of worship was later built nearby, often as not the well and any existing temple, sacred stone or tree were simply rededicated by Welsh saints – probably following a policy of 'if you can't beat them, then join them'.

Many of the sacred stones have long since disappeared; often broken up and put to practical use towards the building of a nearby house or wall – a fate that also befell a good number of castles following the English Civil War, and many monasteries too at the time of the Reformation in the 16th century.

It is no exaggeration, probably, to say that sacred wells in Wales numbered well over a thousand and that in medieval times pilgrimages were a part of life. The Reformation, however, forbade what were then regarded as 'superstitious' practices, with a few notable exceptions; St Winifred's at Holywell in north Wales being one. There, Catholics were joined by Protestants, the latter of course only valuing it for its medicinal properties while the priests of the former attended surreptitiously.

The rituals performed at the sacred wells were varied and the cures – given that not all were medicinal – must have often owed much to faith, as well as a variety of mysteries long discarded by our modern philosophies.

Although wells were visited all through the year, Easter (or the pre-Christian equivalent), early summer and Sundays were particularly popular, as was the special day to honour the saint after which a well was named.

The visitor may have come to pray, to be healed, to seek a cure for sick cattle, to have a curse removed – or to make one! Both the last two could be very expensive – the former more so than the latter. At Ffynnon Eilian in Llaneilian-yn-Rhos, the financial gains were considerable and the cursing, curing and collecting became so outrageous that more than one person ended up in prison.

Judging by the repeated mention of cures for them, the population seems to have been excessively plagued by warts. One north Wales man is said to have had thirty-three on one hand alone. As the cure for that particular case was to prick each wart with a pin and then rub it with sheep's wool, one cannot help wondering if such unhygienic treatment rather aggravated his condition – especially as the wool was often gathered from hedges, or anywhere else it could be found without actually having to catch a sheep.

Francis Jones(2) came up with some interesting statistics about cures. Top of his list for warts was Caernarfon. Ceredigion had the most wells associated with the treatment of eyes – a common ailment, closely followed by Pembrokeshire, Glamorgan and Caernarfon. The latter county, together with Meirionnydd, was also well served with waters for the alleviation of rheumatism while Glamorgan was the county in which to live if one suffered from skin diseases.

Many offerings were thrown into wells, including pins, coins, buttons, keys, quartz stones and pebbles, according to the place, the belief, and the cure being sought. Wells acted as fortune-tellers; the behaviour of fish and eels were 'read' as omens of one sort or another. Girls would visit them for signs of the 'tall dark stranger', sometimes spreading their handkerchiefs upon the water to see which way the wind blew it, and any lover who went through the requisite ritual could tell whether or not the future would bring fortune, faithfulness and fertility.

Once the object of sacrifice was placed in the well, it was unlucky to take anything out again, so dissatisfied customers did not get their money back. Monetary offerings did not always get cast into the water anyway, often being conveniently placed in a box provided by the priest or the owner of the well.

In a few places, rags were hung on bushes. Like the crutches often found nearby or in local farmhouses, these were possibly left as proof that the malady had been cured and that dressings and supports were no longer needed. On the other hand, the rags may have been a sign of faith that the cure would work. If, on emerging from the well, it was found not to be so, then another piece of rag could be tied round the afflicted part and removed on the next occasion. An alternative theory was that the disposing of the rags represented the disposing of the disease.

There were more drastic rituals attendant on well cures. These often involved rather unfortunate chickens or cockerels, which were said to cure epilepsy. Strangely, they were also claimed as being able to prevent babies from crying at night; the sacrifice of some fowl apparently being an acceptable price to pay for a night's sleep. As Francis Jones(2) remarked, 'we are in the presence of stark paganism'.

In many cases – or so the tales relate – patience was rewarded. No particular mystery would necessarily be attributed to healing at wells with medicinal properties, and neither should cures on a psychological level be underrated. In other cases, miracles, as they say, take a little longer.

'Off with their heads and other diversions'

Decapitation was a common end for many a saint, and was on occasion their making. Wells were often involved, one way or another. Some heads tumbled downhill like that of St Lludd of Brecknockshire, others were sometimes picked up and carried like that of St Justinian in Pembrokeshire who apparently took his own head away from the well. Writings about well cults seem to depict quite a few saints wandering around carrying their heads. Usually, little grudge seems to have been borne towards the decapitators, although St Cynog of Merthyr Cynog in Brecknockshire was very annoyed at having his head chopped off whilst praying, and walked off with it thus causing the well to dry up as punishment. To add credence to many of these tales, 'blood' was often present at the well. It somewhat spoils the fun to point out that the rusty colour of a chalybeate spring, or an area where there is red soil, could very well account for this phenomenon.

'Fishy business'

In a land of rivers and streams, it is hardly surprising that aquatic occupants, legacies from very ancient beliefs, figured largely as omens. You could be cured or your wish granted if the fish touched you or an eel curled itself around your legs. However, if the resident trout or whatever it was that lurked beneath the surface did not appear, then this did not augur at all well.

'Going to the Devil'

Depending upon the custom at the particular well attended, one could use wells to lay curses by throwing bent pins into the depths; rinsing one's mouth with well-water and spitting it out with hatred; sticking a skewer through a frog (ouch!); carting the well-water away to the victim; making wax effigies; writing the name on slate or paper or, as in the case of Ffynnon Eilian (see Denbighshire) and other places, paying the well guardian to lay the curse for you.

If all this sounds a bit far fetched, it may be worth reflecting on the fact that just after the second world war – which wasn't exactly in the dark ages, after all – a young Anglesey woman who had been disappointed in love threw a pinned effigy into a local well.

'Health and Happiness'

Wells were not all doom and gloom. As will be seen, there was lots of dancing around some of them, not only by fairies but also by mortals who drank sugared water and consumed cakes and ale at the local pub – the latter practice admittedly being sometimes frowned upon.

At a time when there was no television to watch, no computers in front of which to sit for hours on end, and no mobile phones to distract everybody within hearing distance, an excursion to the well and a visit to the hostelry afterwards must have been great fun. Plenty of interesting information in the form of gossip was to be had – much more satisfying than the Internet, probably just as accurate, and faster! Pure water, exercise and good clean air must have been beneficial compared to many present day leisure activities.

CURATIVE PROPERTIES OF THE SPAS

If one asks how long ago a well or spring was discovered, the answer will often be that the Romans knew about it or that it was in use since 'time immemorial'. The latter was an expression used by Dr Wessel Linden who, in the 18th century, waxed enthusiastic about more than one Welsh spa. However, whatever their origins, most spas blossomed in the 'hey day' of the 19th century when 'taking the waters' became fashionable and thousands of visitors arrived, thus necessitating more facilities and accommodation.

People embarking on 'cures' usually committed themselves to an arduous regime which often meant rising very early, drinking pints and pints of water and taking a lot of exercise. The latter probably did not involve going too far afield, considering the need to answer the calls of nature brought about by the amount of liquid consumed, especially if taken without specialist advice for sulphur water had a purgative effect as did saline water, which was a diuretic as well. As the two were often taken together, the results must have effectively cleared the system.

> The saline waters are taken early in the morning, the quantity varying according to the requirements of the patient. In a large number of cases they act as mild evacuants, and their cleansing effect on the bowel is shown by the colour of the motions and the definite reduction in the quantity of matter passed ; this being presumably due to lessened bacterial action.
>
> But it is from the sulphur waters that one looks for and obtains the greatest diuretic effect. Careful observation show that these waters cause diuresis without irritation, even in damaged kidneys ; that is to say, in the so-called gouty kidney and kidney of chronic Bright's Disease.

Depending on the facilities of the individual spa, visitors could bathe, immerse themselves in radioactive mud or, in cubicles equipped like some ancient chambers of horrors, have electric impulses shot through them. After this, if their medical man recommended it, they could also be 'bled'.

Local people knew from experience which spring cured what, how much to drink, and which ones were suitable only for bathing. However by the 19th century this was not enough and spa waters became the subject of much scientific analysis. No self-respecting physician could advise a patient unless he had a complete breakdown of the content of each spring.

Analysis of Saline Spring, Park Spa, Llandrindod Wells.

Analytical Laboratory,
11, Salisbury Square,
Fleet Street, London,
December 2nd, 1869.

My Dear Sir,

I have now the pleasure of sending you the following results, which I have obtained in the analysis of a sample of the mineral water which you sent me. .

An imperial gallon contains:—

Organic and Volatile Matter and Water of Combination	·9·15 grains
Chloride of Sodium	177·39 ,,
Chloride of Magnesium	18·53 ,,
Chloride of Calcium	36·88 ,,
Oxide of Iron and Alumina	0·70 ,,
Sulphate of Potash	2·30 ,,
Nitrate of Potash	0·26 ,,
Iodide of Potassium	0·35 ,,
(Containing ·27 of a grain of Iodine.)	
Carbonate of Potash	1·04 ,,
Carbonate of Lime	9·31 ,,
Soluble Silica	1·01 ,,
Sulphuretted Hydrogen	Traces

256·92 grains

This water possesses valuable medicinal properties. It is a Saline spring, and contains an appreciable amount of Iodine.

I am, my dear Sir,

Yours,

AUGUSTUS VOELCKER.

Generally speaking, sulphur water was used for the treatment of skin disorders, bronchial infections, bladder and kidney ailments, gastritis, heartburn and relative conditions. If combined with saline water, it was also considered effective treatment for rheumatism and gout.

Magnesium was taken for digestive complaints and any ailment of a tubercular nature while chalybeate springs helped remedy problems caused by iron deficiency and did wonders for anyone feeling the need for general 'toning up'.

Barium Chloride was thought to be beneficial for heart conditions but only Builth and Llangamarch Wells appear to have possessed waters with any considerable quantity; the latter being particularly rich in content and gaining quite a reputation because of it.

Bathing in good pure spring water was efficacious – particularly for eyes – and when drunk, it at least had the advantage of tasting pleasant, especially when compared with some evil-smelling sulphur spring.

Visitors to coastal resorts could sometimes avail themselves of medicinal waters. Aberystwyth for instance, once possessed a chalybeate spring of some renown and Swansea, popular for the high iodine content of its sea water had a holy well, situated at St Helen's, which also had chalybeate properties.

'Taking the waters' as a fashion, declined with the Second World War but one can still imbibe at Trefriw and Llandrindod. However, the average visitor, having satisfied novelty and nostalgia, will almost certainly return to the convenience of a bottle of multi-vitamins to remedy any deficiencies in the system.

OLD AND NEW COUNTIES

Old Counties	New Counties
Sir Fôn/Anglesey	Ynys Môn
Brycheiniog/Brecknockshire	Powys
Sir Gaernarfon/Caernarfonshire	Gwynedd/Conwy
Ceredigion/Cardiganshire	Ceredigion
Sir Gaerfyrddin/Carmarthenshire	Sir Gaerfyrddin
Sir Ddinbych/Denbighshire	Dinbych/Conwy
Sir Fflint/Flintshire	Fflint/Wrexham
Morgannwg/Glamorganshire	Abertawe(Swansea),
	Nedd/Port Talbot
	(Neath Port Talbot),
	Pen-y-bont(Bridgend),
	Rhondda Cynon Taf,
	Bro Morgannwg
	(Vale of Glamorgan),
	Merthyr Tudful,
	Caerdydd(Cardiff), Caerffili,
	Blaenau Gwent, Torfaen,
	Cas Gwent(Newport)
Meirionnydd	Gwynedd
Mynwy/Monmouthshire	Mynwy/Monmouthshire)
Maldwyn/Montgomeryshire	Powys
Sir Benfro/Pembrokeshire	Penfro/Pembrokeshire
Sir Faesyfed/Radnorshire	Powys

YNYS MÔN (ANGLESEY)

' . . . the water was perfectly calm; nothing was moving upon it, nor upon the shore, and I thought I had never beheld a more beautiful and tranquil scene.' (George Borrow *Wild Wales*)

Ynys Llanddwyn (small island/peninsula off S.W. Anglesey)
'One of the most exhilarating places off the Welsh coast.' (*Anglesey guide* 1948)

Ffynnon Dwynwen (St Dwynwen's Well)
Dwynwen, daughter of the 5th century king Brychan (whose name is remembered in Brycheiniog), was said to have been in love with a young man called Maelon Dafodrill, but refused to consent to any hanky-panky prior to tying the knot. Maelon, being a man of his own time and many another, found succour elsewhere leaving Dwynwen distraught. The jilted maid asked for help in her prayers and drank a potion given by an angel, which not only cooled her ardour but also turned her unfortunate ex-lover into a block of ice. However, the story ends happily because Dwynwen was granted three wishes, one of which she used to have Maelon thawed out, the second that she should never marry and serve God always, and the third that no true lovers should henceforth suffer because of their affliction. She also moved to live on the island that still bears her name and became a saint. St Dwynwen died around the year 465, maybe, but a Celtic cross in her commemoration was definitely erected in 1903. If you are Welsh and suffering from love, the 25th January is her Saint's day, when help is guaranteed should you send expensive cards to the cause of your suffering.

In the old days the coffers of Llanddwyn benefited greatly from the many pilgrimages made to Ffynhonnau Dwynwen, the shrine and, in the middle ages, a monastery. It was customary to carry a candle when seeking a cure for such things as pleurisy, lung and bone diseases at Ffynnon Dwynwen. However, it was another nearby spring known as Crochan Llanddwyn that was frequented by the lovesick invoking the help of St Dwynwen, patron saint of Welsh lovers. One had to either drink the water or, if the result was

not satisfactory, then jump in, as told in part of a poem by Ceiriog
(J. Ceiriog Hughes 1832-1887):

Mi eis i Landdwynwen ar ddiwrnod o haf
Yn isel fy meddwl, o gariad yn glaf;
Mi yfais o'r ffynnon, ond trois yn ddi-oed
I garu fy nghariad yn well nag erioed.

Gofynnais am gyngor, a d'wedai hen ŵr;
Y dylwn ymdrochi yng nghanol y dŵr;
Mi neidiais i'r ffynnon a suddais fel maen,
Ond codais mewn cariad dau fwy nag o'r blaen.

I went to Llanddwynwen on a summer's day,
Melancholy and lovesick;
I drank from the well, and immediately'
I loved my sweetheart more than ever.

I asked for advice, and an old man
Told me to bathe in the water:
I leaped into the well, sank like a stone,
But arose twice as much in love as ever before.

Here, as in other places (Llangybi, Sir Gaernarfon, for instance),
an eel or fish could foretell luck in love. Handkerchiefs were cast
on the water and in the late 18th century, the portents of fishy
girations were divined by an elderly lady who told one woman
who had seen two fish each coming from opposite directions, north
and south, that she would marry a man from Sir Gaernarfon –
which she did. Perhaps he was from Llangybi!

No walls have been built around the well and, as it is set in the
rocks above the sea, it is not easy to locate – local advice might be
needed before setting out to look for it. It is also advisable to watch
the tide if walking over the sands to Ynys Llanddwyn, otherwise,
you might see more fish than you bargained for.

BRYCHEINIOG (BRECKNOCKSHIRE)

'It tastes strong of sulphur and smells much like gunpowder.'
(Builth Wells Spa, Lewis Morris, 1748)

ABERHONDDU/BRECON

Priory Wells
The Benedictine Priory here, dating back to the 11th century, was valued by its founder Bernard de Newmarche at £112.12 shillings. Fine examples of monastic buildings still remain as well as a 12th century font. It became Brecon cathedral in 1923.

The well, once used by the monks, is situated east of the close on the left-hand side of the path, and above Afon Honddu leading through the woods to Llan-ddew. Originally a holy well where offerings of pins were made, it also served the community by being used to feed the public water supply. Local inhabitants were still glad of it in 1947 during a big 'freeze up' when it was the only water available in the immediate area. Access can be made by crossing a footbridge from the main road on the east side of Priory Hill or via the hill itself against the huge and ancient walls. Both are steep, but the latter enables one to reach this small and rather special cathedral by car. Refreshments can be had at a barn-like structure called, appropriately, 'Pilgrims'.

The well has recently been cleared, preparatory to re-landscaping. An apt choice of plants would be something thorny. Dog-owners seem to have a conscience about allowing their pets to relieve themselves amongst the gravestones, but appear to have rather fewer scruples beyond the gate. Wellsprings Fellowship, who undertook this task, have obtained permission to excavate the well chamber, but this project awaits time – and volunteers who, as they graphically put it, 'have a hankering to examine (and move) the gunk!'

Penginger Well, Penceingaer, Brecon
There is nothing left to see of Penginger Well, which has now been

filled in, and the water piped away. All that remains of the site is an old yew tree. However, the story connected with it is interesting. It concerns St Lludd (also often referred to as Eilwedd, Eluned, Auger, Almedha or Alud). She was said to be another daughter of Brychan (see Dwynwen of Llanddwyn), and destined for martyrdom. It is said that Lludd, a devout Christian, ran away from home to escape the unwanted attentions of a pagan Saxon prince. After trying her luck at nearby Llan-ddew, Llanfilo and Llech-faen and being greeted with varying degrees of hostility, she made her way to what is now the site of Slwch Farm and was welcomed by the then lord of Slwch. The spring below Slwch Tump became Lludd's Shrine, complete with stone chapel.

The pagan suitor, after much searching, eventually found Lludd praying at the top of the hill. Her response was to run away and his was to cut off her head which, it is said, as seems to be the habit of the heads of martyred ladies, rolled down the slope until it hit a stone, where a spring gushed forth. In the 15th century, William of Worcester, a gullible soul, recorded that one could find a hair of the saint on a nearby megalith.

'... as often as anyone in honour of God and the said saint shall say the Lord's Prayer or shall drink of the water of the said fountain, he shall find at his will a woman's hair of the said saint upon the stone by a huge miracle.' One cleric, the Revd Baring Gould agreed that the well was there but much clogged up, and humorously remarked that the 'hair is on the head of the farmer's wife at Slwch' (2).

Not quite as dramatic as the tale of the 'Saxon suitor' is the theory that Lludd made enemies among the various 'pagan' communities which she may have tried over-zealously to convert and that the responsibility for her death might lie in that direction. Certainly, her saintliness does not appear to have stretched to total forgiveness for she placed a curse on the inhabitants of Llan-ddew, Llanfilo and Llech-faen for their inhospitality.

St Lludd was buried at Usk and her chapel destroyed at the time of the Dissolution, that which remained serving as a cattle barn in the 17th century.

Given that there is nothing to see, if you still want to be a pilgrim (St Lludd's feast day is on August 1st), the site is only about a mile east of Brecon. It is on private land but visitors are not unwelcome provided that they follow the country code by closing gates and so on. From Llech-faen, follow the path past Slwch Farm to the third field past the T.V. mast, approaching Slwch Tump (mound) by a wooden gate with stile – a climb that is worth it if only for the view. The well site is below, the hollow occupied by an old tree trunk. There is talk of organising some excavation, but not in the immediate future.

Llanfair-ym-Muallt/Builth Wells

Today, there is nothing about Builth, or Llanfair-ym-Muallt, to help one picture it as the thriving spa it once was.

However, in their hey day, the springs of Park and Glanne Wells were very popular, spouting forth as much chalybeate, sulphur and saline as anyone could wish to drink. The former was particularly good, stronger than the Llandrindod spring and comparable to those in Homburg and Kissingen but not as bubbly, which would presumably have made it less palatable. Containing lithium and barium, it was used for kidney disease, gout and heart conditions. An old guidebook quotes the fact that 'it is now generally admitted that Park Wells' saline waters are quite the best of their kind in the kingdom'.

One local, in a letter of October 1896 said of the Park saline water that it was good when bottled and that he often got out of bed, drank a glassful and went back again, finding it 'a very agreeable way of taking it in cold weather'. It was considered the family medicine and they 'wouldn't be without a jar of it. A powerful apperient but does not gripe' adding that 'it is a very useful injection for piles – an excellent cosmetic and can even be applied to babies for nettle rash' (1).

Glanne Wells, offering sulphurous and chalybeate water, was about a mile and a half to the west of the town on the Cefn-y-bedd road, and Park Wells nearly a mile north-west. The walk along the river to the latter was part of a constitutional recommended to those taking the cure. For the benefit of the infirm, lame – or just plain lazy, waters were made available in the Groe Pavilion in the town centre. Just across the road from the Groe – a pleasant piece of parkland by Afon Gwy (the Wye) – is the old assembly room, now transformed into the Wyeside Art Centre.

In 1748 Lewis Morris, who spent a lot of time sampling the curative properties of wells, wrote about Builth. 'Here is a Well of mineral water at ye Sign of ye Black Lyon noted for curing distempers by washing and taken inwardly is good for asthmas and diseases of ye Lungs, consumptions &c. It tastes strong of sulphur and smells much like gunpowder. About a quarter of a mile out of town there is a Salt Spring called Ffynnon y Parc which produces common salt but not white; about 3 pints of ye water will purge briskly. It tastes a little brackish' (2).

Use of the sulphur water is mentioned in the mid 18th century but the saline was found later by some mowers in 1830 and the brook was named Nant yr Halen (salt brook).

The discovery of the waters meant a boost for Builth, which had suffered considerable hardships over several centuries. Stricken by the plague in the 14th century that resulted in the death of most of its inhabitants, it was almost completely destroyed by fire at the end of the 17th. However, the flourishing of the spa in the 19th century did not result in the building of large houses. Development at Builth was more low key and, once the boom was over, it reverted to what it had been since the 12th century – a small market town. It is these days a venue for tourists and the site of the National Welsh Show Ground is nearby. The pump of Park Wells remains, but that is on private property. The owner is usually quite agreeable to its being viewed and one only has to ask.

Cilmeri

If the wells of Builth have disappeared, one can take comfort in the fact that Ffynnon Llywelyn is not far away – two miles west of Builth at Cilmeri. There is here a monument to Llywelyn ap Gruffudd, Y Llyw Olaf (our last Prince) and down some steps between the memorial and a neighbouring garden, is the well, recently restored.

The story is that the Prince, seeking to avoid detection, had his horse's shoes nailed on backwards so that his enemies would assume that he had ridden off in the other direction, and headed for the shelter of Ogof Llywelyn (cave) in nearby Aberedw. However, he was betrayed – possibly by the blacksmith – and was beheaded by Adam de Francton. Before the head was taken to London, it was washed in the spring, after which undiluted blood is said to have flowed from it for a whole day. Some will tell you that Llywelyn was buried close to Cefn-y-bedd (ridge of the grave) farmhouse nearby – a tale which is much contested. The body probably ended up at the Abbey in Cwm-hir, Radnorshire but that is not a subject to be debated here.

Ffynnon Cwm-twrch, Cwm-twrch, Ystalyfera.

Situated in the far south-west of the county (A4068 just north-west of Ystalyfera), this is a good strong sulphur well, the kind which you smell before you reach it and, like that at Llanwrtyd, it has been dubbed locally as the 'stinking well'.

In the late 19th century, those seeking cures for kidney disorders, erysipelas and rheumatism and the like came from neighbouring counties in large numbers to visit Ffynnon Cwm-twrch.

The well, once the property of Colonel Fleming Gouch, was donated for public use at the end of the first world war, after which it suffered the neglect that befell many wells until, in the 1970's, it was the subject of analysis by Dr D. Thomas who assessed it's considerable sulphur content. By 1993, the local authority was taking an interest and their Public Health Officer recognised the value of the water, adding a few more complaints to the list of ailments that it might cure. The locals have some of their own claims, including baldness (a reputation which is also held by Marcroes Well, Glamorgan). If there is any truth in this, it is surprising that no one has bottled it for commercial purposes. Perhaps Ystalyfera Community Council, in whose care it has been since restoration in 1993, might consider putting it on the market.

Llangamarch Wells

Around 1830, during an unusually dry summer, a cotter went looking for water for his pig and came across a spring that was normally covered by the river. It apparently tasted foul – always a good sign for a cure – but it is not recorded whether the pig drank any.

The mineral properties were tested and the locals used the spring for rheumatism, scrofula etc., the water being eventually channelled into a well and a bathhouse built.

Llangamarch Wells turned out to be almost unique, having water that contained a large quantity of Barium Chloride – a property only then known to be found in such large quantities in Kreuznach in Germany. Beneficial for cardiac conditions, its discovery prompted articles and letters in the 'Lancet' in 1896 extolling its virtues and recommending it for other ailments as well, including fibrous tumour of the uterus, sallow complexion and languid circulation.

Kreuznach or no Kreuznach, one of the visitors in 1912 was the Kaiser and his family, discreetly recorded in the hotel register as 'Prince and Princess of Muster from Germany'. There is no longer access to the spa but the natural local water is so pure that the Lake Hotel has it piped in off the mountain in addition to the mains supply.

Llanwrtyd Wells

This was the southern-most of the chain of mid Wales spas, of which three were in Brecknockshire. The place was originally no more than a hamlet called Pont-rhyd-y-fferau and now, under qualifications that are not quite clear, refers to itself as the 'smallest town in Britain'.

This little town sprung up during the mid 19th century to meet the demands of visitors seeking the cures. People from Merthyr Tudful and other parts of the industrial valleys, agricultural workers from the south-west and many others took the stage coach or, after 1868, the train from Swansea to sample the waters.

The sulphur water is said to be the strongest in the country. One doesn't have much difficulty in believing this – you have only to walk along Afon Irfon and the smell is unmistakable. At one time, when the spring belonged to Dôl-y-coed Hotel, you could get access to the well through a rather ramshackle outhouse. It was an awe inspiring, creepy experience, peering into this large encrusted wellhead and enhaling the stench. If afflicted with an over-imaginative nature, you could easily reach a state of expecting the devil himself to emerge from it at any minute. Dôl-y-coed is now a private dwelling, so such exciting fantasies are denied one. You have to be content with standing by the river these days, and sniffing.

The fame of this sulphur spring as a really effective cure is attributed to a local vicar, the Reverend Theophilus Evans of Llangamarch Wells, although its healing properties were generally known as far back as the 14th century. Be that as it may, nearly all accounts tell the same tale of his encounter with 'the frog'. Apparently, the unfortunate cleric suffered badly from scurvy in 1732 and, being led 'by the nose' to the spring, was too horrified by the pungency to risk experimenting with it until he set eyes on a frog. The creature was swimming around quite merrily and the Reverend Evans, thus encouraged, embarked on the 'cure', which was successful beyond all expectations. Being a gentleman of letters (he was a well known author on Welsh Antiquitaries), he soon publicised his experience.

In 1774 it was decided to find the actual source of the water and, after much digging through a foot of black turf and dark clay, it was discovered that the spring did not, as was thought, come up through the under lying layer of gravel, but flowed from a bog! Off putting though this may sound, the sulphur water was said to be consistently pure, sparkling and easily digestible. Depending on one's intake, which had to be considerable, various skin diseases could be cured within a few weeks. It is said that our reverend friend's condition healed up after two months. The water was also said to be good for both kidney and nervous disorders.

Originally called Ffynnon Ddrewllyd which means 'Stinking Spring' – hardly an attractive name for an up and coming spa, it was understandably later changed to Dôl-y-coed, once the water had been diverted into a well and some bath houses had been put up.

Opened on the Queen's Diamond Jubilee in 1897, the Victoria Wells – also sulphurous – were less grand than their name suggests. Fame caught Llanwrtyd on the hop – some of the buildings were of corrugated iron and some of wood with rush or straw roofs. However, no one appeared to mind and the Welsh speaking visitors who frequented them made sure that there was no lack of home brewed entertainment within to compensate for the rigours of sampling what was on offer in the way of a cure. Chalybeate and saline water were also available – thousands of gallons of the latter being conveyed from Builth Wells some fifteen miles away.

Adequate accommodation was eventually provided and the buildings in Llanwrtyd Wells are really all that remains of the spa atmosphere today. They seem to be sheltered by the mountains so that, unlike Llandrindod Wells (of which more, later), they are not incongruous against the landscape. There are still bogs of course only these days, no one is searching for sulphur water in them. Instead, they hold what they are pleased to call the World Bog Snorkelling Competition and organise Real Ale Walks as an alternative to spa cures. An enterprising little town is Llanwrtyd – but, after all, they have to fill all that 19th century visitor accommodation somehow.

PATRISHOW

Ffynnon Isho

In the Vale of Ewyas (or Llanthony Valley) amidst the Black Mountains on the B4423 which runs from Llanfihangel Crucornwy (north of Abergavenny) to Hay-on-Wye, there are some fascinating little places of worship (including the amazing leaning one called 'Cwmyoy').

Turning left, south of Llanthony, you eventually come to the church at Patrishow said to be founded in the 11th century, which has a holy well set above Nant Mair (brook). Past references indicate that it was held in much esteem and the water is still used for baptisms. Approach to the well is indicated by a Maltese cross marked on a stone of ancient origin (possibly that of a medieval pilgrim), moved from a bank higher up in the 19th century. It is said that a grateful pilgrim, cured of leprosy by the holy water, left a 'hatful of gold' to build the church and amazingly, in the 1960's, a Mrs Durant reported seeing cloths tied above the well, an ancient sign of appreciation for a cure still persisting in this remote place (4). Alas, not all visitors showed their gratitude for the benefits received. The unfortunate St Isho, who had a cell near the stream, came to an untimely end at the hands of a traveller for whom he had cared. The original church was called Merthyr Isho and as 'Merthyr' can mean both 'martyr' and 'saint's burial place', it is likely that either translation is apt.

This is a beautiful, peaceful and isolated place, but quite a challenge to reach. There is no village and a quantity of steep narrow lanes, especially the last one to the lych-gate.

SIR GAERNARFON (CAERNARFONSHIRE)

'Arfon...... is the most rugged and truly alpine district in Wales.' (3)

Ffynnon Cegin Arthur, Llanddeiniolen (situated about five miles (8km) north-east of Caernarfon.
It is possible that the Welsh word *Cegin* in this context could be translated as a 'ridge' rather than the modern translation of 'kitchen'. Certainly 'times long past' is an appropriate description, for this spring appears to have been in use by the ancient Brythons and might have been a Druidic holy place. One of the later beliefs attached to it is that the stone steps leading to the bath were blessed by St Beuno.

This chalybeate spring was very popular at the beginning of the 19th century as coaches ran twice a day during the summer to transport people from what was then Felinheli (Port Dinorwig) station. At one time visitors could submerge themselves in a full-length bath but after a while, drinking alone became the norm and the receptacle for bathing was covered up.

A difference of opinion arose in the results of analysis of the water in 1858. Dr A. Wynn Williams of Caernarfon, who cured many patients here, maintaining that there was about eight grains of carbonate of iron per gallon while Dr Sheridan Muspratt of Liverpool could only find just over three and a half grains. However, a fellow Liverpudlian, one Sugden Evans came up with seven and a half grains and – as far as Dr Williams was concerned – honour was satisfied.

Apparently, the amount of carbonic acid gas was so great that it could be seen, according to Dr Williams, to be 'escaping' from the well itself. Most English waters produced about sixteen cubic inches per gallon whereas that of Cegin Arthur measured twenty-six. Miscellaneous and perhaps uninteresting information one might think – but not to those who had to drink from the well. Rather like adding lemonade, the more gas, the more it masked the taste of the water, and it also avoided any resultant nausea. For this reason it was best drunk immediately, before it went flat. The spring was said to cure scrofula, rheumatism, sciatica, neuralgia, consumption, kidney disease, anaemia, epilepsy, bronchitis, eye conditions, indigestion and depression. It is also said to have cured a sick pig – of what it is not clear, but there are enough ailments from which to choose. The dose was usually half a pint at regular intervals. If, however, one took the waters for too long – the average cure was about three weeks – the result could be a rush of blood to the head!

T.R. Roberts (1) remarks 'There can be no doubt that given a little enterprise on the part of the inhabitants, this well has a glorious future before it.' The inhabitants do not appear to have taken advantage of its potential but one can still visit the place and for its condition and directions, one cannot do better than quote from information given by the Welsh Wells Society.

' . . . In a plantation of trees between the villages of Penisa'r-waun and Dinas Dinorwig . . . following the road from Penisa'r-waun in the direction of Gors farm before turning into the woods and following a track. The trees have covered the spot and little is left now but a square chamber built of bricks in the ground. The well chamber is dry. It is quite small and allows room for only one person to stand in it at a time.'

Aberdaron: Ffynnon Fair, Uwchmynydd, Llŷn

You can only sample the water from Ffynnon Fair at low tide as it issues from the rocks in the bay beneath Mynydd Mawr, below the site of the church. This well has several ancient tales attached to it, mainly concerned with the carrying of water without spilling it. One such is that of a lady of some beauty who had a secret desire. While sitting above the well, she was approached by a spirit in the form of a woman who instructed her to go down to the water and, if she could carry some up the steps and around the church without spilling any, her wish would be granted.

A variation on this ritual was that, provided the wish was neither mundane nor covetous, a mouthful of water brought up to the church would also do the trick – but not if it was swallowed or spilled. Another version is that the water had to be carried in the palm of the hand, which would certainly not be easy.

Capel Mair or Tŷ Mair was said to have been built for the use of sailors and the imprint of the saint's hand and the shape of one of her horse's shoes is said to be found in a rock near the well.

Ffynnon Gybi, Llangybi (Llŷn) (approx. 3 miles (5km) north-east of Pwllheli)

Ffynnon Gybi has been much used over the years, its healing properties being said to cure warts, blindness, scrofula, rheumatism and lameness. Crutches and wheelbarrows were recorded as being left nearby from the beginning of the 18th century. The well was owned by a William Price of Rhiwlas in 1750 who, after the persuasions of the Reverend Williams of Llanystumdwy that its properties merited consideration, had a bath house built. His faith was not misplaced. In 1767, Dr Wessel Linden published 'An Experimental and Practical Enquiry' finding the water to be beneficial for ophthalmic, scrofulous and nervous afflictions, and the spring at Llangybi was said to be equal to any other in the country.

There is a record of a case of blindness in the register of cures from 1766 when Siôn Rhydderch, who had lost his sight some thirty years previously, recovered it after bathing his eyes regularly for three weeks. A local tailor named William Siôn Thomas is also recorded as having been cured of a 'pain in his nose'. The Saint was still revered and sick people often ignored the mineral properties, preferring to evoke the intervention of St Cybi instead.

New tenants of nearby Tynyffynnon had to pay an incoming fee of three pounds five shillings to the outgoing one, ten shillings of which was in respect of the land alongside the well and the rest for 'llawr y ffynnon' which represented the 'well ground' rent.

The water was used for bathing and drinking, and people also filled containers for use at home. Not everyone wandering around the locality carrying casks was necessarily returning from the well, however. One story tells of a group of 18th century smugglers carrying spirits from Porthdinllaen who, bumping into a customs officer, claimed that they were on their way to the above mentioned Mr William Price with water from Ffynnon Gybi.

One of Ffynnon Gybi's legends was that of the sacred eel – a large specimen that lived in the well. If it curled itself around the sufferer's bare legs, a cure was certain unless, like one unfortunate girl, you were so terrified that you collapsed and died on the spot. Great consternation was caused by a man who took the eel out of this well, many people being convinced that the healing properties had gone with it.

In the 19th century lovesick girls performed the same handkerchief ritual as is mentioned in connection with other wells. Here, floating northwards was a sign of bad luck in love, but floating southward augered well. If no handkerchief was available, a feather or even a rag sufficed. One poet, disapproving of such superstitious behaviour, was moved to verse.

Ambell ddyn, gwaelddyn, a gyrch
I bant goris Moel Bentyrch,
Mewn gobaith mai hen Gybi
Glodfawr sydd yn llwyddaw'r lli.

Some folks, worthless folks, visit
A hollow below Moel Bentyrch
In hopes that ancient Cybi
Of noble fame blesses the flood. (1)

The well is sited below Llangybi church, at the eastern end of which is a stile. Once over this, the path leads to the opposite corner where there is another stile, from where you then make your way down the side of the field. Alternatively, there is a footpath (signposted) from the road. In addition to two well chambers, there are the substantial ruins of a cottage and the remains of a toilet building across the brook. A stone causeway approaches the wells. Too enthusiastic an investigation can result in getting rather muddy, especially in inclement weather.

Ffynnon Fyw, Mynytho, Llŷn (B4413 west of Llanbedrog)
Situated at Horeb Congregational chapel, Ffynnon Fyw has recently been restored. In times past when it was valued for its cures, it was very impressive. There were two wells – a small one

31

for drinking and a larger one for bathing.

Entrance was through a huge oak door with 6' (1.8m) high walls, and there were two bathing areas – one which was approximately 6 feet (1.8m) by 9 feet (2.7m) and the other 3 feet (.9m) by 5 feet (1.5m). Stone seats were set against the wall and steps led into the well. Much store was set by the water as a cure for blindness and skin diseases. Curig, to whom it is believed to have been dedicated, had a chapel near the well.

Llandudno. Haulfre Gardens

Looking at the large seaside town of Llandudno today, it is hard to imagine the resort as it once was – barely a village with just a few fishermen and miners' cottages nestling under Penygogarth (the Great Orme). One of its sources of water was fed down from a well in what is now Haulfre Gardens, on the hillside above.

This is not a holy well. No fairies danced here, no pins, as far one can ascertain, were dropped into it and neither did it oblige with curses or cures but it has a little tale associated with it and although neither mysterious nor exciting, it is interesting because it is contemporary and has the advantage of being true.

At the site stands the Haulfre Gardens Café with magnificent views over the town and bay. It was originally opened as a café by Lloyd George in 1929 – and while name dropping, one should mention that the place was once part of the estate of Thomas Tipton, that well known purveyor of tea – a suitable name to be associated with the present enterprise.

When the tea gardens were bought by Joan and Michael Edwards a few years ago, they knew nothing of their extra acquisition until their surveyor mentioned the well for insurance purposes. It was discovered about eight feet (2.4m) beneath the kitchen floor with some of the pipes, which had taken the water to the village until 1887, still intact.

With all the copper mining in the area, it is probable that there are quite a few wells below the surface in various places. Deeds for this Haulfre Gardens site alone show a hundred rights for copper, although not all were explored.

Mr Edwards is now busy researching its history. He has built two steps by which, if energetic, one can lower oneself into this fascinating little grotto.

You can have an excellent tea at the café and admire the view but the well is not accessible to the public. That may be a project for the future, however. Meanwhile although it may no longer serve the community at large, the well continues to be of use – because its temperature is a constant eight degrees, Mr Edwards finds it an ideal store for his wine!

Trefriw (B5106 in Dyffryn Conwy)

It is claimed that the springs at Trefriw, which issue from a cave, were first discovered by the XXth Roman Legion sometime between 190 and 250 AD. Of course, it is likely that the local inhabitants had known about them centuries before the XXth Legion ever came here to mine for minerals, but the fact is not recorded. A landslide engulfed the cave at some point, and it remained covered until the mid 18th century when Lord Willoughby de Eresby unearthed it and built a primitive bath house in 1743. This is an impressive piece of architectural achievement of the Cyclopean Quarry variety, which apparently means that it is built of dry stone (no mortar nor cement was used), and is held firmly balanced on a central stone by the invisible means of its own weight.

Visitors can still see this old place with its solid, enormously heavy, slate roof. One room has a huge slate bath and the other has, among other things, an elbow bath. The cost for full body immersion lasting four minutes in the 1930s was, apparently, four shillings (which was rather a lot). It was, understandably, proportionately less to soak the affected parts in the special hip or elbow baths.

There were originally three springs discovered in the cave. There was the sulphur water immediately opposite the entrance which was used for drinking, and on the left for bathing. However the one on the right was the most impressive, having very strong iron properties. In 1833 Robert Owen found that the head of the sulphur mine had filled up but, once it was cleared, a very forceful gush of water resulted and local inhabitants began using it for skin diseases, rheumatism and stomach conditions.

A second bath house was erected in 1863 by the trustees of the estate, and the supply of bathing water increased. Earthenware and glass pipes conveyed the waters to the pump room where they were dispensed through glass taps. After this a charge was made for the 'facilities'. The drinking water was not separated from that for bathing!

The water rights were acquired by a local company in 1873, which built more substantial pump and bath rooms. Demand became such that a door had to be knocked through to the old building so as to create extra baths, which could be filled overnight to satisfy the next day's requirements. Later when a sense of decorum (or should that be prudishness) took over, the two rooms were set aside for ladies and gents respectively.It must have been an improvement on bathing in the cave, which had been the previous practice.

Dr O.O. Roberts of Bangor, a gentleman of many longish words, praised the Trefriw water at great length saying, among (unbelievably) much, much, more that it was of:

'inestimable value in the successful treatment of that numerous and obstinately troublesome class of diseases whose Protean powers depend upon a deranged state of the nervous system, caused by a proportional inequality or deficiency in the blood of those inorganic elements which are indispensably required to render the assimilation of nutritive inorganic substances available for the healthy sustenation of the animal machine'.

The comments of a Dr Hayward in the 19th century amount to the same thing, but are rather easier to understand.

'As sulphate chalybeates are the best of all chalybeates, the Trefriw is the finest chalybeate water in Great Britain.' Certainly it is good strong stuff. One piece of advice given in the 19th century recommends washing the mouth out after drinking it, 'to avoid the blackening of teeth'.

This water did much good for 'mineral poisons' found in lead mine workers. When one considers the amount of lead mining that went on in the 19th century, especially in the area around Trefriw itself, the well must have been very important. The ailments included lead constipation, copper epilepsy, mercurial eczema, arsenical eczema, loss of teeth, paralysis, trembling, phthisis, ulceration, colic and palsy. In these enlightened days, when we are so preoccupied with pollution and the sinister effects of working with potentially dangerous substances, this list gives one pause for thought . . .

As its fame increased, Trefriw water was bottled (there is an example of a hand-operated bottling machine in the 'Victorian Room') and shipped all over the world at a cost of forty-two shillings for two months supply. One assumes that this price was beyond the means of the average lead worker but, hopefully, there was still access to the spring at not too high a charge.

Following the 19th century boom, Trefriw, like most spas, lost its appeal and closed in 1952. Happily, it re-opened in the 1970's and welcomes many visitors all year round. There is a tearoom and garden in which you can enjoy snacks in summer and winter, a car park and a half-hourly bus service. It you fancy a ride on the train from Blaenau Ffestiniog or Llandudno, you can alight at Llanrwst station and catch the bus to Trefriw.

Not unreasonably, there is a charge if you want to follow the trail and visit the magical cave, complete with stalactites. You can drink the 'iron' water from the rock by using the disposable spoon provided, and without any noticeable blackening of the teeth or exceeding a 19th century recommendation of a 'tablespoon to a wineglassful twice or thrice a day'. You proceed at your own pace on a self-guided tour, pushing the appropriate buttons for information. The tour has six stages, some being outdoors, and is very informative, including miscellaneous gems such as the fact that the Romans fished Afon Conwy for pearls. It also draws the visitors' attention to some large T-shaped slabs that are now believed to be ancient 'Directional Stones'. They were formerly part of the steps up the path until spotted by knowledgeable members of a guided tour in 1987, and henceforth dug out and removed to the side of the pathway.

Trefriw has done some impressive marketing. The shop offers all sorts of health giving goodies including sachets of the water – trade name 'Spatone iron+' for which they have not only succeeded in getting national outlets including some main branches of Boots and various health food shops, but also offer a mail order service. Before dismissing this as a gimmick, there are some facts that should be considered. One problem is getting the right quantity of iron into the system. A lot of it, like many things consumed in tablet form, goes out as one might put it 'with the wash'. Any amounts that remain, when concentrated, can cause side effects. Trefriw spa insists that its water contains no additives, is a 100% natural iron food, and is normally in the blood stream within about half an hour of ingesting.

Trefriw has had its share of poetical praise, one from a lady who was injured in a car accident and cured from insomnia by the waters. Of the many ailments previously listed, that one was not to be found, but presumably must now be included.

To Trefriw Wells, a lady came –
(Her nerves all shattered) – old and lame,
Her joy of life and spirits spent,
Her days were just one long lament.
Against the wretched motor man
Who knocked her down within a span.

This shock to nerves caused sleeplessness;
The broken arm gave hopelessness;
With bruises, cuts and all contusion
She listened to her friends' effusions,
To join them in the loveliest·spot
That loving nature e'er begot.

To drink the water from the Wells,
(Which pain and anguish, quickly quells)
She came. She drank. The baths she tried
And sleep returned, so long denied:
Had she the ready writer's flow,
This wondrous cure all men should know.

Today's visitors may not be given to such eloquence but there is little doubt that this is a place worth praising not only for its attractive situation but because, thankfully, much effort has been made to ensure the survival of the spa.

CEREDIGION (CARDIGANSHIRE)

'As the bowels should be attended to in commencing a course of the chalybeate spa, a glass of sea water or any physic may be taken previously.'

T.J. Llewelyn Pritchard, 1824
(on Aberystwyth chalybeate spring)

ABERYSTWYTH
Of the Chalybeate Well in Aberystwyth, an 1824 guide book says:

The nectarious stream will bring
Tincture and lustre to the eye, the lip,
And give an irony strength unto the frame . . .

Well, not any more because they went and built a railway yard over it However, this spring, discovered accidentally in 1779, was once a considerable attraction to the area, but was replaced by sea bathing, of which more later.

Most guidebooks, extolling the virtues of spa water, concentrate upon its curative values. However the Aberystwyth one of 1848 went a little further than that, discussing the way in which the water loses its properties with

THE CHALYBEATE WELL.

Exclusive of the convenience and excellence of the bathing at Aberystwith, it possesses, like Scarborough and Brighton, an advantage over many other places on the coast, that of having in its immediate vicinity a fine Chalybeate Spring, the use of which is applicable to, and will much assist in the cure of many diseases for which the sea is visited. This Well was discovered by accident about the year 1779, and is situate a few hundred yards east of the town, upon a common close to the mill leet, and not far distant from a stone quarry.

Some years ago, when the water was directed from the mill leet, for the purpose of clearing away the weeds which had collected there, the Well became dry, and a small stream proceeding from the north was observed rising from the bed of the mill leet. Upon covering this over, the flow returned at the usual place.

The neighbouring country abounds in springs of a ferruginous nature, and traces of sulphur have been lately discovered at Penglaise, the seat of Roderick Richardes, Esq.

This Spa yields about one gallon in a minute. After rain it runs much faster, and its specific gravity at the temperature of 56 is equal to that of distilled water. During the months of March and April, the temperature varied from 46° to 50°. and did not rise higher when that of the atmosphere was above 60.*

Before sun-rise, when the degree of heat was 42, that of the Well continued 47—Fahrenheit.

'different re-agents' such as:

Tincture of gall affords a fine purple approaching black
Syrup of violets, after standing some time, becomes very
                                        slightly green
Tincture of litmus becomes changed to a light red colour
Volatile caustic ammonia and caustic potash occasion yellow
                                        sediments
A solution of soap is curdled both before and after it has been
                                        boiled

Were the mid 19th century visitors really interested in such things?
The old guides also mention, quite incidentally, that the spring only had a saline taste after high tide, when it had been mixed with seawater. How sad that in these modern days of polluted oceans, such a statement would give us considerable pause for thought before sampling it.

Times have indeed changed as the following excerpt from a 1980 edition of the Cambrian News shows ('Born on a Perilous Rock', W.J. Lewis).

In 1807 it (the beach) had four bathing machines for women near the end of Pier St and two for men at some distance to the north. In 1826 there were 21 such machines but there were complaints that there was no awning to protect the bathers from the public gaze. This beach was also used on occasions by country people from the mountainous districts inland. A report of 1806 suggests that they had no qualms about mixed bathing. 'Natives of both sexes among the mountains are much addicted to sea bathing during summer nights . . . On reaching the beach they strip and take a promiscuous plunge without any ceremony. This kind of ablution is generally taken on Saturdays in order that they may rest on the following day!'

Would this stand for what is now popularly known as *skinny dipping*, 1806 style?
However, decorum was not entirely lost. An 1827 guidebook

praises the convenience of not having the bathing machines make 'the tedious descent of many hundred feet on a sandy shore before the temporary inhabitants can arrive at a sufficient depth of water. When the tide is in, the longest distance requisite to roll the machine exceeds not three yards'.

The building which stood over the spring was demolished around 1868, but there is a Chalybeate Street to remind us of its existence, although this is not in fact situated near the site. One may still take the 'promiscuous plunge', and the good air off Cardigan Bay remains as beneficial as ever.

Ffynnon Gloch, Llanarth, near the Church (4 miles/6.5km S.W. of Aberaeron on A487)

There is a spot near Ffynnon Gloch upon which a spell was said to be cast. Long ago, says the legend, the devil stole a bell from Llanbadarn Fawr and stopped by the well to rest. Since that time the place has been under a curse – it being said that anyone standing on it can no longer hear church bells ring.

Ffynnon Gybi, Llangybi (A485 north-east of Llanbedr Pont Steffan/Lampeter)

The water of Ffynnon Gybi, near Llangybi church, was said to cure aching limbs, rheumatism, sore eyes, scrofula and scurvy. It was also a 'comfort stop' for pilgrims en route to Llangeitho. Tradition has it that the site of a nearby house called Llety Cybi was used by St Cybi, but Edward Llwyd referred to the well as Ffynnon Wen (2). 'On Ascension Eve they resort to Ffynnon Wen; after they have washed ymselves at ye well, They go to Llech Gybi yt is an arrows flight from ye well. There they put ye sick under ye Llech, where, if ye sick sleeps, it is an infallible sign of recovery: if not death.'

How long is an arrow's flight? Seemingly about two hundred yards (towards Llanbedr Pont Steffan/Lampeter) up Bryn Llech (slope) to Llech Cybi (a large cromlech). The old custom was still in existence as late as 1911.

SIR GAERFYRDDIN (CARMARTHENSHIRE)

'The place of the holy well was taken occasionally by a pool . . . at Llanpumsaint five pools in the river were regarded as the pools of the saints commemorated in the place name.' Francis Jones (2)

Carreg Cennen Castle Well

About three miles south-west of Llandeilo on an unclassified road near Trap is the impressive 12th century castle of Carreg Cennen, perched high on a limestone crag overlooking the valley of Afon Cennen, some 300ft/91m below. The wishing well in the cave is still to be seen. Originally, pins were thrown in but any subsequent rituals are unclear.

The ancient and atmospheric natural hollow beneath the castle is accessible only through a 200ft passage from within the walls. A legend claims that Owain Lawgoch sleeps there with his troops, waiting the trumpet that will arouse them all to rid Wales of the invading Saxons. Myth or no myth, one can imagine the value of the well to those defending this impressive place, hundreds of years ago. The castle and the well are open all year, except Christmas Day.

Llwyndewi

Also near Trap, is Llwyndewi where there is a spring of unusual purity. The bottled 'Brecon Water' comes not in fact from Brecon at all, but from this spring at Llwyndewi – its reputation thus transferred to another county which seems a little unfair on the ancient Sir Gaerfyrddin. This is, however, considered to be justified on the grounds that it is in the area of the Brecon Beacons National Park.

Nowadays, there is little of note in the way of medicinal springs but this is a region much noted for cures. Not far away is the little village of Myddfai whence came – or perhaps one should say 'come' for there are those today who claim to have inherited the power – physicians and healers going back many centuries. Their authenticated cures are documented in a manuscript from medieval times, which is now kept in the British Museum.

Middleton Hall, Llanarthne Wells (B4300 west of Llandeilo)
The chalybeate spring here was once much in use with both hot and cold baths nearby. When Sir William Paxton owned the land in the 19th century, he ordered an analysis to be carried out that revealed, among other things, an iron content of five grains per gallon. It was fairly strong stuff, but because there were 16 cubic inches of carbonic gas to the gallon to mask the taste, it was not unpleasant to the palate.

The spring is now situated in the very impressive National Botanic Garden of Wales, which is a successful millennium project. Supported by substantial grants from many quarters, it is certainly more than an ordinary public garden. The size and scope it covers are not for detailing here – enough to say that it has seven lakes, a glass house of 110 x 60 metres, a theatre and, of course, plants and woods galore. The chalybeate spring and an old holy well can be seen in the Pont Felin Gat area.

DENBIGH

' . . . A well' said she, 'by the road side, which in the time of the popes was said to perform wonderful cures.' George Borrow 'Wild Wales' (in the Llangollen valley)

Ffynnon Fair, Botryddan (Bodrhyddan) Hall (A5181, 3 miles east of Rhuddlan)
Ffynnon Fair in the grounds of Botryddan Hall near Rhuddlan is in very good condition. Its covering is an octagonal structure crowned with a pelican, apparently representing part of the coat of arms of the Conwy family, and there is a rectangular pool beneath. You can no longer get married there as is said to be the custom in the old days, when any couple wished to tie the knot in secret. There is a distinct possibility however, considering the proximity of Ffynnon Fair at Botryddan to the one at Cefn Meiriadog (see below), that some couples were going to the wrong well when they came to Botryddan! The latter also lacks the atmosphere of many of the old wells, some of which exude that special feeling of discovery when one comes across them. However it is all very decorative and pleasant as one would expect from something situated in the tasteful gardens of a stately home. One does not 'discover' Ffynnon Fair, but pays to view the delightful grounds and house on Tuesday or Thursday afternoons from June to September.

Ffynnon Fair, Cefn Meiriadog.
One well that was definitely used for marriages is another Ffynnon Fair, this one situated in the Cefn Meiriadog area. On the A525, approaching from the south, turn left after the bridge over Afon Elwy (about 2 miles/1.6km south-west of Llanelwy/St Asaph) and left again into the first lane.
Peter Roberts in his book Cwta Cyfarwydd mentioned clandestine marriages at this well from as early as 1640, including those of three daughters of an Evan Lloyd, one of whom married a Thomas Wynn from Llanrwst. A local notary records seven marriages there during the mid 17th century. It is not certain whether these were legal, but a clergyman from St Asaph could,

presumably, be persuaded to undertake the ceremonies after dusk.

The holy well, approximately 8ft (2.4m) square, had without doubt already been in use for very many centuries before it is said to have been rebuilt, together with an attractive chapel, around 1500. Like many other wells, it became much neglected at the end of that century. As it was considered to be a healing well (mainly used for eyes and infertility), there would almost certainly have been some sort of covering or shelter in the vicinity at one time.

The water is very cold and the spring that flows into the well is recorded as rising at 4000 gallons (18160 litres) an hour in documentation from the late 20th century.

Interest in Ffynnon Fair has revived and it was excavated in 1963. The poet, Gerard Manley Hopkins commented with great favour upon his visit to the well where he 'said a prayer and drank the water'. If he could not run to putting his praise into verse, then this service had already been performed by Felicia Hemens (possibly best known for her 'The boy stood on the burning deck), a poet and playwright who moved to north Wales from Liverpool, and who wrote as follows:

'Fount of Vale! thou art sought no more
By the pilgrim's foot, as in times of yore,
When he comes from afar. his beads to tell,
And to chant his hymn at our Lady's Well,
There is heard no Ave through thy bowers
Thou art gleaming lone midst thy water flowers.
Fount of the Virgin's ruined shrine!
A voice that speaks of the past is thine.
It mingles the tone of thoughtful sigh
With the notes that ring through the laughing sky.'

Ffynnon Sara, Derwen
Ffynnon Sara is about half a mile/800m south of Derwen, on the left hand side of a minor road when travelling in a northerly direction towards Derwen and Clawddnewydd, and to the north of the A494. At this point, the road dips and there is a sign to Braich Farm. There is a stone plaque at the gateway and a path to the well.

Possibly originally dedicated to St Saeron, this well was also known as Ffynnon Pylle Perl, the pools of the same name being found nearby. Situated on the old Pilgrim's Way which ran from Tyddewi (St David's) in the south to Ffynnon Gwenfrewi at Treffynnon (Holywell) in the north, Ffynnon Sara was a 'pin well', the water of which was used for bathing and recommended for rheumatism, skin diseases and cancer. The nearby cottage where the crutches were left was burned down in the mid 19th century, but the well not only still exists but was lovingly restored in the 1970's by the local rector.

Ffynnon Degla, Llandegla

Ffynnon Degla (off the A5104 just north of the junction with the A525 approximately 9 miles/15km south-east of Rhuthun) is certainly a well that one feels to have 'discovered'. It is not easy to find, and it is difficult to improve upon the directions given in Denbighshire County Council's *Discover Medieval Denbighshire*.

'Starting from the church (and after asking permission at Mill Farm), go through the aluminium gate to the right of the row of cottages, past farm buildings, and then over a stile by the next gate: this is a public right of way. After the second gate, bear right off the footpath and walk across a field towards the stream until you reach a low bank. Turn left along this bank to find the unobtrusive well – a sunken stone trough – between the bank and the stream'.

A bit of a challenge maybe, but it looks more complicated written down than it actually is 'in the field'. What is certain is that many people found their way to this well at one time. Francis Jones (2) gives the dimensions of the well as 4' by 3' (1.2m by 90cm) and about 1' (30cm) deep, and the well chamber as 7' by 5' (2.1m by 1.5m). Ffynnon Degla was believed to cure epilepsy as well as what was then known as King's Evil, better known today as venereal disease, and continued to be visited for cures far into the 19th century. Excavation in 1935 revealed quantities of pins, coins, pottery as well as white stones and quartz, the latter probably being an indication of ancient pagan rituals. In the drought of 1921 it proved also to be of practical use by providing the locality with water.

I mentioned, in the introduction to this book, the use of cockerels and hens at some wells, and Ffynnon Degla was one such. The ritual here involved, walking three times around the well on a Friday evening, carrying a cockerel (or a hen if the epileptic was female) in a basket whilst chanting the Lord's Prayer (three times). The unfortunate fowl was then pricked with a pin which was then tossed into the water. The sufferer (with his/her pin-pricked cockerel/hen) had to spend the night in the church (after also walking around that three times whilst again chanting the Lord's Prayer) under a carpet beneath the Communion Table, with his/her head resting on the bible. At dawn he/she blew into the cock/hen's beak, thus supposedly discharging the disease. The poor fowl was then left in the church, in the hope that it would die and thus signify a cure. This, one imagines, would rather depend upon exactly where, how deeply, and how carefully the pin was stuck. This is not a custom about which to read while eating supper, and was roundly disapproved of by the Rural Dean who tried to get it stopped in the mid 1700's. However, he was defeated by claims of cures – and monetary considerations possibly played some part. From 1699 to 1743 the parish clerk received donations – one groat per ritual to the poor box and a second groat to himself followed by a further gift, this time of silver, again to the poor box. Perhaps it was more than coincidence that the parish sexton's own son took part in the ritual around 1813 seeking a cure for epilepsy, and doing no harm in keeping the firm going, so to speak.

Cockerels were reported to have been seen staggering nearby after such rituals as late as 1850 – after all, being used as a pin cushion would be enough to make any self-respecting bird unsteady. The practice did not begin to die out in Llandegla until the mid-19th century, and continued in various forms in other parts of the country until later even than that.

To end on a different note, one might return to the name, and fate, of St Tegla. She, according to a second century document, was a disciple of St Paul and lived in what was the then equivalent of Turkey. It is a little strange that this lady, who was apparently martyred (almost a pre-requisite for sainthood) at the honourable age of ninety, should be remembered with a feast day in September every year in the county of Dinbych? Someone, somewhere, without any doubt, will know why.

Ffynnon Eilian, Llanelian-yn-Rhos

At Llaneilian-yn-Rhos (near Colwyn Bay) there was once a famous – or perhaps that should read 'infamous' – well. Situated near the parish church, it was, until the latter part of the 18th century, simply another holy healing well. Dedicated in the 6th century to St Eilian, various rituals were performed there that including cursing and lifting petitions, but these became not only more sinister but also more and more financially rewarding.

Around 1800, the owner was said to acquire a handy income of about three hundred pounds per annum from charges made for laying on curses and for removing them. At that time people paid Sarah Hughes, an elderly woman who lived nearby, and who kept a written record, and then threw a pin in the water. On receipt of further remuneration from the victim, she would take it out again. In spite of the efforts of the authorities, she seems to have evaded any criminal charge.

Others followed, and one John Edwards did get his just deserts when he served a gaol sentence of a year in 1820, this being the consequence of charging an Edward Price fifteen shillings for the removal of a curse at the well. Presumably, Price was one of the few prepared to tempt fate by contesting the matter. Perhaps he had fallen into very bad luck and therefore contended that the lifting of the curse hadn't worked and that nothing worse could befall him in seeking redress.

However, these were small fry compared with the super con-man, the 'priest' Jac Ffynnon Eilian – actually a tailor by trade – who set up a very lucrative business in 'cursing' and 'lifting' from 1820 onwards. He was sent to prison in 1823 and in 1829 the well was closed up, it's water diverted to the river and that, thought the local residents who had been doing their best to deter visitors by denying the well's efficacy, was that.

However, they reckoned without the persistent Jac who reappeared on the scene after his gaol sentence and, finding that the spring still existed, started up all over again. But by 1831 he

47

was back behind bars. This time it was for lifting a curse on the husband of Elizabeth Davies who paid him nineteen shillings for the service. An insight into Jac's rogueishness is indicated by the fact that, when tried, he offered in recompense to put a curse on the man who had laid the first one – which Mrs Davies did not accept.

Jac died, having repented of his sins, in 1858, but 'cursing' continued around the site, wells opening and closing intermittently. Such beliefs did not easily wane. There is,for example, the strange tale of a farmer who, during the period after Jac's death, consulted Ffynnon Eilian about the identity of the thief who had taken his grain. This turned out to be his own sow whose strange behaviour, on his return from consulting the water, gave her away!

Francis Jones (2) gives a fascinating account of the rituals and activities that were performed at Ffynnon Eilian. These can be summarised as follows:

The fees were originally one shilling for cursing and ten shillings for lifting. By 1820, they had risen to five shillings and fifteen shillings respectively and in 1831, as mentioned, the charge for lifting was nineteen shillings.

The following describes the methods that were used at Ffynnon Eilian. For the laying of curses, the victim's name was recorded in a book and initials were often scratched on a slate which was put into the well. A pin was dropped into the well or stuck through the victim's name in a book. The guardian of the well would then read Biblical passages before the applicant took a cup of water, drank some, and had the rest poured over his/her head. This was done three times while the applicant uttered the form he or she wished the curse to take. On other occasions, pins were stuck in wax effigies, to which copper was then attached. Secret cursings followed, before the effigy was dipped three times in the well, and then left at the bottom.

To lift the curse, the victim had to read or listen to psalms. He/she would then walk three times around the well and read further portions of the Bible. The guardian emptied the well and gave the 'accursed' the appropriate slate. Apparently, 'something in Latin' and about 'ab Eilian' was muttered during the

Ynys Llanddwyn

Surviving Monastic buildings (now the Deanery) Brecon Cathedral

Brecon, Priory Well, Brecon Cathedral

Llanwrtyd Wells (Brecs) Sulphur well (early 1900's). Note bottled water on right.

Bridge over Afon Irfon, Llanwrtyd Wells.

Dôl-y-Coed Wells, Llanwrtyd, in it's hey day.
(It was originally called Ffynnon Ddrewllyd – 'Stinking Spring')

Builth Wells (Brecs) Park Wells (early 1900's)

Builth Wells (Brecs) Glanne Wells (early 1900's)

The Llywelyn stone at Cilmeri.
Llywelyn's spring is nearby

Llangammarch Wells

Ffynnon Cybi, Llangybi.

Roman Wells at Trefriw

Trefriw (Caerns) Full bath, hip bath, elbow bath in old bath house.

Trefriw (Caerns) Close up of scales.
The notice reads
'To WEIGH oneself OFTEN
Is to KNOW oneself WELL
To KNOW oneself WELL
Is to BE WELL'.

Trefriw (Caerns) Hand operated
bottling plant
(on view in Victorian Room)

Trefriw (Caerns) Entrance to Spa (2000)

Trefriw (Caerns) Slate bath (on view in old bath house)

Llandudno Haulfre Gardens exterior – Michael Edwards.

Ffynnon Fair, Dyffryn Clwyd.

Trefin (Pembs) Village pump (1999)

Trefin (Pembs) Village well (1999)

St David's Cathedral

St Non's Well, near St Davids (Pembs)

Font in St Non's Chapel

Present Day St Non's Chapel

Llandrindod Wells (Rads) Rock Park Spa (early 1900's)

*Llandrindod Wells (Rads)
Rock Park Spa (1999)*

*Llandrindod Wells (Rads) Rock Park
Spa Chalybeate Spout (1999)*

Llandrindod Wells (Rads) Pump House (1810)

Llandrindod Wells (Rads) Pump House Hotel (1850)

Llandrindod Wells (Rads) Pump House Hotel (1930's)

*Llandrindod Wells (Rads) All that survives of the Pump House Hotel –
the boiler room.*

Glen Usk Hotel, South Crescent, Llandrindod Wells.

Llandrindod Wells Park Pump Room in its heyday.
Small orchestras played in the pavilion (left).

Rock Park, Llandrindod Wells Spa (after 1970's restoration)

Pump House Hotel, Llandrindod Wells.
It had accommodation for 1st and 2nd class visitors.

proceedings. Having returned home the victim had to read, on three successive Fridays, the Book of Job and the Psalms. A bottle of well water had to be drunk over a period of three nights and the 38th Psalm also had to be read.

As Francis Jones pointed out, the large amount of money charged for lifting the curses shows how strong was the belief in the power of Ffynnon Eilian. Nor was this belief confined to the uneducated. A non-conformist minister became very ill because he believed he had been cursed there and an eminent professor born in 1872 recalled that when he was a child, the expression 'I'll put you in Ffynnon Eilian' remained a common threat.

Perhaps it is a relief to know that proper destruction of the well was finally achieved and no one is any longer in danger of being cursed at Ffynnon Eilian.

Ffynnon Ddyfnog, Llanrhaeadr-yng-Nghinmeirch. (On the western side of the A525, approximately half way between Rhuthun and Dinbych)
Following the path by the church tower alongside the brook, one reaches the well by the side of which St Dyfnog is said to have lived in the 6th century. The spring issues from a rock and tumbles into the well below.

Much visited from very early times, the water from this well was purported to alleviate skin irritation and scabs. Some were even convinced that it cured the 'pox', which was a rather remarkable claim.

Writing at a time when there was much Protestant scepticism, one unknown poet swore by the miracles of the spring saying that they cured those who were deaf and dumb by the powers of St Dyfnog. Such miracles had apparently been made possible by his unusual penance of standing in the powerful stream of water, attired in nothing more than a hair-shirt and with a rather kinky iron chain around his waist.

The well's popularity in the 18th century resulted in the provision of a marble paved bath and some buildings (which were decorated with tiny figures), together with other necessary conveniences. As is often the case, the well buildings have long gone, but the bath survives.

The large number of pilgrims attracted to the well contributed greatly to the wealth of the church including, it is said, the wonderful early 16th century Jesse window. There is fascinating information available about the treasures available within, many of which are probably linked with the 'holy water'. As it is nearly always open, a peek inside is certainly worth the trouble.

SIR Y FFLINT (FLINTSHIRE)

' . . . not with prayers or with holy masses, but in every species of frolick and excess . . . celebrated by persons of our own religion only (Protestant) who flock here on that day for most unsaintly ends.' Pennant 1796 (2) on Ffynnon Wenfrewi.

Ffynnon Wenfrewi, Treffynnon (St Winifred's Well, Holywell)

Ffynnon Wenfrewi or St Winifred's Well at Holywell is recorded in rhyme as one of the 'Seven Wonders of Wales' and the town, as both its Welsh and English names suggest, grew up because of it. It was widely known throughout Britain with pilgrimages reputedly being made here from as early as the 7th century. The well was in Norman hands for a century and a half or so, after the Countess of Chester granted it to the St Werburg Monastery in 1093 but, by 1240, Dafydd ap Llywelyn bestowed it upon Basingwerk Abbey in whose hands it remained until 1537.

Many titled people made pilgrimages to St Winifred's and it was sometimes favoured by the English monarchy. Richard I visited it in 1189; it seems probable that Henry V did so in 1416, and that Edward IV followed in both their steps. Financial assistance towards the cost of a priest was granted by Richard III and in the 15th century the Countess of Richmond built an ornate gothic chapel over it. In 1686 James II and his queen went to the well to ask that a son be born to them and, wonder of wonders, a son was born in 1688.

Known as the 'Welsh Lourdes' for it's miraculous cures, the well inspired many a bard and painter, and sketches and engravings of it were popular throughout Britain. As has been said previously, the well of St Winifred even managed to survive the Reformation because the chapel was too famous and, more to the point, far too lucrative. The sum of ten pounds was received in offerings at the well in 1535 alone but, for a while at least, the Protestants gained little from it. The Catholics endeavoured to get their hands on the money by soliciting offerings in boxes that were then taken into the well chapel. The assembly was told that it was better to give the money to them rather than the king – a practice that the lessee, not unnaturally, did his best to stop. As Protestants and Catholics congregated in their thousands, the powers that be decided that, for the most part, it was better to turn a blind eye to the religious rituals and sit back and take the money.

However, 'big brother' was always 'watching'. A record was kept of the numbers and names of Catholics who turned up on St Winifred's Day in 1629. The consequence was that the Chief Justice of Chester issued orders – which he attempted to enforce – to prevent any further pilgrimages. In 1637, the iron posts around the spring were removed and the image of St Winifred 'spoiled'.

Undeterred, the Jesuits set about building a house for pilgrims in 1642 but this was thwarted by the authorities. However, by the end of the 17th century, things seem to have become quite lax. Celice Fiennes wrote in 1698 that the bathers 'walked along the stream . . . then came out but there was nothing to shelter them', adding that although they are 'exposed to all the company . . . the Religeuse are not to mind that'. She went on to report 'an abundance of devout papists on their knees all around the well' which conjures up an interesting picture, depending upon one's interpretation of the word 'exposed'. In 1796 on the first Sunday after St James's Day, it is recorded that there was 'frolick and excess' but not, apparently, by the Catholics.

Besides healing skin diseases and almost every other condition, St Winifred's was also said to detect crime. One amusing story (2) concerns the theft of a goat – which the thief had eaten – bleating from his stomach, thus establishing his guilt. 'What a dreadful thing!' comments the report. 'This which is denied by a rational creature with an oath, is revealed by a brute, and what is more unusual, by one already eaten.'

The legend of Gwenfrewi/Winifred belongs to the 'headless' category. She was the daughter of Teuth, a nobleman, and had been tutored in Christianity by her uncle, St Beuno. The perpetrator of the crime was one Caradog, the son of another nobleman from nearby Penarlag, who was obviously not used to rejection, and chased after her from the church and beheaded her.

A spring appeared where her head fell which, for three days afterwards, produced milk. St Beuno laid Gwenfrewi's head back on her shoulders and her life was miraculously restored. With a scar round her neck, she then led the contemplative life of a nun and seven years later, it is said, moved to Gwytherin near Llanrwst, where she was buried. And what of Caradog? Well, he just disappeared into the ground – sent to the devil by the curses of the irate St Beuno.

The moss where the head lay gave off a fragrant smell and her blood spotted the stones, the stain of which her uncle promised would never be washed away and as the waters ebb and flow, this can be seen – according to an anonymous poem of 1823 which tells of the blood of the beheaded Winifred on the stones in the well.

Ar y cerrig yn y ffynnon
Mae y gwaed yn amlwg ddigon
'Rhwn a gollad Winiffreda
Pan ga'dd ei phen ei dorri yma

Upon the stones in the well
The blood is obvious enough
This that Winifred lost
When her head was chopped here

Medieval writers mention three stones, each with red spots that appeared to move with the flow of the water. The rusty stains of chalybeate water or red soil often offer a simple explanation for such phenomena and at the same time rather spoil such legends. G.A. Cooke in his 1827 *Typography* puts further dampers on it, going as far as to say that 'a person of this place' recollects the stones being taken out and painted red in order that 'some degree of sanction might be given to the tradition'. He also claimed that the legend itself was invented by the Basingwerk monks in the early 14th century.

The well at one time yielded a great deal of water, and was measured at as much as 4,000 gallons a minute. It was somewhat controversially used to power several 19th century mills that stood nearby. Mr Cooke states that the spring rose in a 'long basin 12' by 7' and 4' deep containing forty tons', and that it broke out with 'great rapidity discharging 22 tons of water in a minute'. It is no longer so productive but still impressive and worth the small fee to visit it.

MORGANNWG (GLAMORGAN)

'Each morn, benign of countenance,
Upon Glamorgan's pennon glance . . . '

Ab Gwilym's 'Ode to Glamorgan'
as quoted by George Borrow in *Wild Wales*

Pen-rhys (Off A4085 to the north-west of Pontypridd)
This well is referred variously – according to religious belief and
period – as Ffynnon Pen-rhys and Ffynnon Fair. Its reputation in
medieval times was very high indeed, so much so that there was a
chapel, accommodation for guests, a hostelry and various other
buildings around the site. During the 19th century local farmers
used the water to make good butter.

These days, the view below is no longer of tranquility and
woodland but a valley full of industry and housing estates; the old
pilgrim's route has been replaced by a new road and one has to use
a certain amount of imagination to recapture the atmosphere of
olden times. However, it is wondrous enough just to ponder on the
fact that some of the infirm were actually carried up to this well.

The water was believed to cure rheumatism, skin diseases, eye
disorders and deafness. Pin throwing was popular, this being done
after the visitor had washed in the well. Discolouration of the pin
was a portent of success. However, as the Reverend Tissington, a
19th century cleric remarked, there were always 'scores of pins' in
the water, and one wonders how anybody could recognise his or
her pin among so many.

Still, the well was the subject for many a Welsh bard. Gwilym
Tew said in the form of a cywydd in the 15th century:

'I will go to Pen-rhys
In my one shirt
For fear of ague
Bearing on my knee
At the appointed time for a pilgrim
A taper, a fathom long.'

Writing in the following century, Lewys Morgannwg praises the glories of Pen-rhys and the statue which stood there that was said to have miraculously appeared from an oak in ancient times. He goes on to extol sufferers to 'cast your disease upon the Maid', calling upon the blind to believe 'he shall see day', that cripples 'will find their feet and run' and that 'they will hear if they be deaf'. Here, asserts Lewys, the dead were brought back to life and the mad received baptism.

These small extracts are mere translations of the original Welsh and can only partly convey the intensity of feeling conveyed by the writers.

Alas, the statue to which Lewys Morgannwg referred was carted off to Chelsea and burnt on instructions from Oliver Cromwell. That it should have been a victim of the Reformation is an indication of its importance. A letter to Thomas Cromwell from Bishop Latimer, dated 13th June, 1538, expresses the hope that the 'sybyll' will be bestowed to 'sum good purpose' having brought 'many to the eternal fyre'. It ends with the comment that, together with the statues at Walshingham, Ipswich and Doncaster, they would 'make a jolly musture at Smythfield' and that they would 'not be all day in burnynge'.

The removal of the Pen-rhys statue had to be undertaken in great secrecy for fear of an uprising and on September 26th of that year, the unenviable task fell to one William Herbert.

In spite of the destruction of the statue, the holy well continued to be visited but by the early 19th century, the original site of the shrine was barely discernible and the well was in a very poor state.

However, the story has a happy ending. In 1939 Rhondda Borough Council started to take some interest in what was by then their property and railed off the well and the little stone building over it. The war intervened but on September 12th, 1947, about four thousand Catholics made pilgrimage to Pen-rhys. Still, little progress was made in saving the well for several decades.

Meanwhile, 'Our Lady of Pen-rhys', as the statue is now known, was destined to rise out of the ashes through the generosity of Miss M.M. Davies of Llantrisant who had a replica carved in oak and set in nearby Ferndale church. This lady also owned the land upon which the original statue had stood and she decided to give it to the Archdiocese of Cardiff. In 1953, with the help of contributions from many Catholic organisations, the statue was rebuilt in Portland stone as near in resemblance to the original as was possible.

The resulting pilgrimages were impressive. The first brought over twenty thousand people which proved to be both gratifying and perplexing because such a large number at one time was more than could be dealt with. The well was also still being restored, this work not being finished until the mid-1970s. It did, however, include the installation of piping to facilitate access to the water. At last, all being complete again, a thanksgiving service was held at the well on June 8th, 1977.

This Catholic shrine sees pilgrimages from many other denominations these days and the way up the mountain is no longer arduous – unless one chooses to go on foot. Interestingly, walking uphill and down dale to this holy well via the ancient route was revived as a three-day exercise at the end of May in 1995. The trek, with diversions to other sites including the holy well at St Gwynnos, covered thirty-three miles and revealed some beautiful countryside. It started at Llantarnam Abbey (the monastery which at one time owned the well), and proceeded westwards by stages with, for those who joined at the beginning, two overnight camping halts. Such was the success of the venture that the event was repeated the following year.

However, the well at Pen-rhys can be approached by a less demanding route. North-west of Pontypridd, turn right onto the B4277 from the A4058 (Maerdy/Aberdare road) and then left after about a mile/1.6km, towards Ystrad. Pen-rhys is on your left. Of course, the sense of achievement will not be as great as that which one feels after a three-day walk. As the Western Mail commented on the 1996 trek 'Pilgrimage is good for the soul'.

ABERTAWE A GŴYR
(SWANSEA AND GOWER)

Caswell

The holy well at St Peters was excavated in 1895 when there was apparently no surface trace of it at all, the bank being covered with trees and the ground around being marshy. However, a trace was eventually found and it was evident that there had once been an arch built over it. It appears that the well escaped the fate of many others during the Reformation, being abandoned rather than destroyed and was subsequently used by the Baptists.

T.R. Roberts writing in 1897 mentions a spring issuing from Caswell rocks and wonders at the fact that, even though covered by the sea at high tide, the water was pure again once the sea had receded. If this was a spring gushing from a vertical rock, then this fact is hardly surprising. However if the water came up from a flat surface, and there are many on the Gower, then it was probably worthy of mention.

To go back to St Peters; the history of the well does not appear to have any unusual stories attached to it. However, the ruins of the nearby chapel and priest house can still be seen from an adjacent path.

Llanrhidian

This is the home of the only EEC approved mineral water in Wales. It is a fossil spring that emerges through sandstone at a nearby farm. Owing nothing to rainfall, the spring maintains a constant flow and the temperature remains at fifty-two degrees Fahrenheit winter and summer.

The spring, owned by a well established independent family business called 'Gower Spring Water', is not open to the public. The water – which contains no toxic substances and reinforces the immune system – is not available through supermarkets, but can be purchased from selected stores (which once included Harrods and Harvey Nicholls) and at Swansea Tourist Office.

Oxwich

People once bathed in the holy well here, but it disappeared in the 19th century. There is, however, a story associated with it. This is one of the *ceffyl-dŵr* (water-horse) tales concerning a white horse walking on its hind legs, which was seen by the vicar and his son. The beast went along the path. entered the well and never reappeared. Not surprisingly, the local people were scared to go near the place after dark.

Unfortunately, there is nothing to be seen now. Two cliff falls, the first in 1855 and a second in 1872, disposed of both the church and the spring.

Abertawe/Swansea

Swansea was a really popular resort for cures, but relied mainly on its seawater. This contained (and possibly still does, but now mixed in with a few unmentionable things no doubt) high quantities of iodine. Many visitors were attracted here in the 19th century and the town sported a bathhouse on the sea front as well as horse drawn bathing machines.

However, in G.A. Cooke's *Typography* (3) written around 1830, the following appears:

'The only mineral spring in the county is at Swansea, which has an acid styptic taste like alum, though the predominant salt is a vitriol. It turns blue with vinegar, but will not curdle with milk. A gallon of this water yields forty grains of sediment, of a highly acid, styptic, vitriolic taste, and light brown colour which will ferment with spirit of harsthorn, and oil of tartar. It is recommended in a diarrhoea, and will stop blood externally, where applied to wounds.'

T.T. Roberts in 'Spas of Wales' (1897) refers to a Swansea Spa near the town with highly medicinal properties and this is no doubt the medieval holy well at St Helens, a little to the west. This spring was chalybeate and external application was deemed effective for ulcers, wounds and cancer. The chalybeate content was said to be 'fairly strong'.

In the mid 19th century, the curative properties of St Helen's Well were set to verse telling of a tearful 'William', who, having visited the well with an ailing leg, lived on 'until May Day'.

I gyrrau Abertawe
'Aeth William fardd mewn dagra
Wrth wthio'i glun i ddyfroedd byw
Fe gafodd fyw hyd Clama.'

One can only hope that his visit was in June so that the poor soul survived at least another twelve month,.

The well which, according to the County Archivist, stood roughly at the junction of Catherine Street and St Helen's Avenue, was still visited in 1955 but it had more or less dried up by the time a sewerage system was laid in Bryn-y-môr Terrace.

Whether Mr Cooke's spring is the St Helen's Well, it is difficult to be certain. His description certainly sounds as if the water was 'fairly strong' but the St Helen's water fermenting with spirit of Harsthorn and oil of Tartar would be more of a matter for a chemist to confirm. With no reference to any other well in Swansea, one is probably safe in concluding that they are one and the same.

Taff's Well (about 10 miles/16km north-west of Cardiff off the A470)
Ffynnon Daf, also once known as Ffynnon Dwym ('heated well' for it was thermal), lies on the eastern bank of Afon Taf. It is one of the many wells known to and used by the Romans, and bathing in it was said to cure rheumatism and ailments affecting limbs.

The well was given a shelter of corrugated iron, behind which the bathers could divest themselves of their garments. Gentlemen hung their breeches outside to alert the ladies of their presence while the latter hung something similar (probably their petticoats rather than their bloomers) for the same purpose. A lady dressed in grey and surrounded by lightening was said to haunt the well – perhaps she was searching for some missing underwear.

At around Whitsuntide in the 19th century, it became fashionable for youngsters to splash the well water over each other before going off to dance nearby.

The well has now been bricked up but the door to it can still be seen in the park.

MEIRIONNYDD

'During the bathing season this place (Aberdyfi) is well supplied with provisions, and cheap so that many genteel families frequent it . . . ' (3)

Ffynnon Fihangel, Blaenau Ffestiniog.

Ffynnon Fihangel, situated at Congl-y-wal, was popular until the end of the 1800's among those seeking cures for rheumatism, broken limbs and various other maladies, and was visited as late as 1914. The well, which was six-sided and accessed by two steps has unfortunately disappeared under rubbish and rubble. However, the spring flows bravely on through iron pipes which once conducted it from it's source under a cottage floor. Indeed, all may not be lost and this particular well may emerge from beneath the ruins if the local council has it's way. Efforts are being made to obtain grants for it's restoration, which one hopes will eventually be successful.

It is thought possible that Ffynnon Fihangel may be the original sacred well of Ffestiniog but, not being associated with any saint, it was as often as not referred to simply as 'Y Ffynnon'. The land belongs to Mrs E.W. Hughes of Ffynnon Manod, Blaenau Ffestiniog (Tel. 01766 830113) from whom permission to visit can be obtained.

Ffynnon Sulien, Corwen

St Sulien came with St Cadfan (of Tywyn) and others to Wales from Brittany. To confuse matters, there was also a later Sulien, a medieval vicar 'Iorwerth', to whom there is a monument.

The well is close to the old mansion of Rug. It is some distance from the parish church and about a mile/1.6km from Corwen. The well chamber measures 9' (2.7m) by 6' (1.8m) and is over 4' (1.2m) deep. It is built of stone slabs and has steps leading down to it. Constructed at an early period, this continuous flow of cold, pure water would have been invaluable to local inhabitants and Ffynnon Sulien was once considered more sacred than the nearby Afon Dyfrdwy (River Dee). Indeed, the well water was actually carried over the river to the font at Corwen for baptismal purposes. It was believed to be good for chronic rheumatism, but analyses appear to be hard to come by. Sufferers were possibly cured by shock for, if you dip your toe for long in this still, full well, then you will undoubtedly get very 'cold feet'.

Ffynnon Drillo, Llandrillo (B4401 to the south-west of Corwen)
The interesting tale about this well, which in times past stood approximately 500 yards/450m from the church and was much used to cure various ailments, is that it is purported to have appeared in different places. One story is that it dried up because someone threw a dead animal into it. Another was that, in the middle of the 19th century the farmer, on whose marshy meadow it was situated, would not permit strangers to visit it and that St Trillo himself intervened (it is said that it once had a stone alter nearby), and caused it to spring up on another farm instead. The fact that such waters often 'moved' due to varying conditions of the soil or rock from which they spring need not spoil the story, of course.

MYNWY (MONMOUTHSHIRE)

'Treleg wells of late years have been found very Medicinal and of the Nature of Tunbridge flowing from an iron ore mineral.'

Nathan Rogers 1708 (2)

Chepstow Wells

In the Chepstow area, there were once two wells which are worth mentioning. Both were of the 'ebb and flow' variety. One was near Bridge Street and the other at Pwll Meurig, $1^1/_2$ miles/2.4km to the south-west and situated in the north-eastern corner of Mathern House. St Tewdric's had, according to an 8th century legend, a large log of 'magical' qualities which was beneficial to those who stood upon it while washing their faces. The log would be born out to sea and return again within four days. A local man, anxious to put this phenomenon to the test, buried it but it was back on the fourth day just the same and the sceptical meddler died within a month. To spoil the fun, there is a mundane explanation (if the Severn bore can be dismissed as merely mundane) for it is this which took the log out into the ocean on the ebb when it flooded the well. As for the sceptic – perhaps wet feet brought on pneumonia.

Ffynnon Efa, Eveswell, Maindee, Newport.

There is a ghost story connected with this well. It concerns an Eva Roberts and the account is given by Fred J. Hando (4).

Apparently, she was the daughter of the postmaster of the little marshland village of Whitson and for reasons which appear unknown, returned to haunt her father. The poor man was driven to gathering the local people together – complete with the requisite 'bell, book and candle' to have the ghost exorcised. However, Eva made an appearance before the proceedings had really commenced and was chased by the village folk out of the marshes and up to Maindee where she inexplicably dived into the depths of the well, vanishing for good. The well was re-named after her to commemorate the event.

TRELECH

The Virtuous Wells

These were situated some seven or eight miles (11.5 to13km) north of Chepstow on the B4293, and about a mile/1.6km south-east of Trelech, in a meadow on the left hand side of the Tintern road. They were very popular as early as the beginning of the 18th century, for the cure of eye disorders, indigestion, women's ailments, scurvy, colic, hypocondria and skin diseases, and were said to be most effective if taken early in the day after fasting. The waters were favourably compared with those of Tunbridge Wells. Indeed, although the good folk of Trelech were undoubtedly extremely virtuous, the adjective in the well's name is thought to have described the purity of the water's properties, not the morals of the local populace.

Trelech, like a lot of holy wells, is thought to have been used by the Celtic Druids. It was much visited in the 18th and 19th centuries, attracting many pilgrimages. There were several springs here – most reports mention seven – but by the mid 20th century only four remained and these dwindled to one, this being 'St Anne's well' which for a while was in a sorry state. An early 19th century writer, W.H. Thomas, commenting upon what he called 'this neglected fountain' upbraided the proprietor, suggesting that he should 'rebuild its ruined walls' and 'cleanse out its channels and invite guests to a festival of health'.

The wells featured among Trelech's 'Three Wonders', the other two being a tumulus and three large megaliths. Trelech (meaning 'stone or slate town') is thought to have been named after the latter – known as 'Harold's Stones' which are probably of Bronze Age origin but, nevertheless, have an unlikely tale associated with them that they commemorated a victory by the Saxon King Harold.

Among the rituals at the wells was the casting of pebbles, and subsequently hoping for plenty of bubbles to result. The success of the cure or wish was commensurate with the amount of bubbles and if there weren't any at all, the caster was disappointed, if not exactly doomed. Margaret Eyre (4) in 1905 describing this 'virtuous' well 'spoken of as St Anne's Well by people who did not belong to Trelech' commented 'I afterwards learnt that I ought to have dropped in a pebble and wished as it fell through the water'.

The basin into which the spring runs is Medieval. It is set in the back of a stone walled chamber the sides of which, complete with stone benches, curve towards the entrance, which is accessed by steps. Two square niches are set in the wall on either side of the well, probably for offerings or to hold drinking vessels.

Fairy magic was said to be wrought at Trelech, particularly on Midsummer's Eve and Halloween. The little people were said to go there to dance and drink water, and they used hairbells as cups. These would be found discarded around the place the next morning. Local folk carefully collected them, leaving them to dry after which they were stored to treat certain ailments.

It is said that a local farmer who scoffed at the myths surrounding the well once destroyed a fairy ring, whereupon the water ceased to flow at his farm. An old man met him at the edge of the spring and told him that this was punishment for his misdeed, whereupon the farmer replaced the grass and remade the ring, thus ending his personal drought.

Some tales connected with the Trelech wells are more sinister. One concerns the suitor for a fair maid who, unfortunately and unbeknown to him, was the daughter of a witch. The mother, like many another, did not approve of the affair and set about casting spells to be rid of the unwelcome blip on her horizon. Her intention was to drown him in the well whence he was dispatched, in spite of the pleas of the daughter, to fill the kettle. His evil future mother-in-law was meanwhile brewing the spell in her saucepan. Whilst bending to reach the water, the young man found himself pulled in, tugged from beneath and pushed from above. He managed to struggle to the surface three times and freed himself from the invisible force on the final attempt. He returned to the cottage with a full kettle and was greeted with a look of horror from the witch who was still busily stirring her evil brew. From the pot emerged a ghastly laugh with such force that the lid shot up the chimney, leaving him in no doubt as to her intention. He sensibly fled, never to return.

St Anne's well was restored in 1951 to commemorate the

Festival of Britain. There are very recent instances of its being 'dressed' with decorations in the niches, and with rags on the nearby trees, all proving that the age of superstition, belief, enchantment – call it what you will – is, happily, not yet dead.

MALDWYN (MONTGOMERYSHIRE)

'Meifod is celebrated in Welsh poetry because here, or nearby, there was once a summer residence of the princes of Powys.'

Blue Guide to Wales

Llanfyllin (A490)

Ffynnon Fyllin was also known as Ffynnon Coed y Llan, and is situated in a beautiful spot some three hundred yards/270m west of Llanfyllin church. It was restored and reconsecrated in the 1980s.

In the 6th century, Saint Myllin is said to have baptised converts here, immersing them fully in the water, a practice that was unheard of until then. Being constantly in the water, he earned himself the title of 'Sant mewn llyn' (the saint in the lake). It was the custom to visit the well on Trinity Sundays when sugared water was drunk, the local maidens standing the 'treat'. The men's contribution was to supply cakes and ale at the Tynllan pub afterwards. It was a healing well with rags being dipped in the water and then hung on bushes. Fortunes could also be told at Ffynnon Fyllin as well as the granting of wishes, provided that the wet rag disintegrated on the branch!

Ffynnon y Clawdd Llesg, Meifod (south of Llanfyllin on the A495). Sometimes known as Pystyll y Clawdd or Ffynnon Spout.

Of the many wells in this area, several were visited for medicinal purposes. Of these, the still existing Ffynnon y Clawdd Llesg was the most well known – together with an adjacent spring that was said to cure eye afflictions. Clawdd Llesg was primarily used for the treatment of scrofula, with sufferers instructed from an inscription over the spring that 'every wound … be held for twenty minutes under the spout three times a day'. Instructions were also written on the walls of the shed erected in the mid 19th century. There is a record of a young man suffering with a tumour in his nose coming some distance to seek a cure here, and one cannot help wondering at his difficulties and discomfort in exposing this part of his anatomy to the water for twenty minutes.

Up until the early 19th century, local inhabitants made visits here on Trinity Sunday, when they drank sugared water and afterwards repaired to the nearby alehouse known as Yr Hen Dafarn. Two local ministers attempted to stop the custom but the local youth continued to go to the well on the eighth Sunday after Easter and danced the day away on the grass.

Instructions were not all that were inscribed on the walls of the building. In 1898 a F.W. Elmore wrote 'I found health here' and verses were also carved including the following *englyn*.

> Yn y lle hwn ni chewch wellhad – oni
> Wnewch uniawn ddefnyddiad,
> Ac erfyn ar Dduw cariad
> Heb rith am ei fendith fad.

> In this place you will not find health - without
> making proper usage,
> And praying to the God of love
> Without guise for his good grace

Notably, this is a Protestant verse – unelaborate in its expression as is another in English:

> Lord grant us from this little brook
> Thy crystal water clear
> To wash our souls and heal our wounds
> While we are lingering here.

The writer, returning to the well after an absence of twenty-six years, found his poetical effort obliterated. He therefore carved it again with a note to that effect 'I wrote this verse for the first time in 1873 but I now again visit the place and I find it vanished and I write it again G.G. Nov 1899'.

Ffynhonnau Penegoes (3 miles/5km east of Machynlleth on the A489)
One of the three Penegoes wells is called Ffynnon Gadfarch, named after St Cadfarch, patron of the church. The well, situated in a

nearby field, was used by sufferers from rheumatism and other pains in the joints.

The other two are close to the school and are situated alongside each other with low stone walls and steps to the water, which is about 2'/60cm in depth. One well is supposed to be colder than the other, presumably because the spring source is deeper. This pure water was taken internally or applied externally. Both were said to be good for a variety of complaints and the place was very popular. Pilgrimages were still being made here in the 19th century and probably later, but no evidence of covering or facilities remains.

After some time, as the popularity of the waters faded, the wells became neglected and 'gunged up'. However in 1980, the local council embarked on the daunting task of literally unearthing them, shifting some twenty-four tons of mud in the process. Thus did Ffynhonnau Penegoes rise again.

PENFRO (PEMBROKESHIRE)

'A Pembrokeshire tradition shows that saints were cantankerous and violent on occasions.' Francis Jones (2)

St Davids and St Nons

Built around 1181, supposedly on the site of the saint's original monastery, the beautiful old cathedral of Tyddewi/St David's, with the Bishop's Palace nearby, stands in a secluded river valley. Unfortunately, there is nothing left of its two wells, the water from which was diverted to run into Afon Alun. This was done in 1866 when it was discovered that the foundations of the building were being damaged by the water running beneath. One of these wells was situated at the east end and the stream ran through the crypt of the original college chapel. Records suggest that it may once have been known as Ffynnon Fair and later, Pistyll Dewi. The story goes that when Afon Alun ran dry and the monks short of water, St David went away to pray and Pistyll Dewi was the result – and rather useful it was too, producing not only water but at times, milk and wine.

However, you don't have to go far to reach St David's birthplace – or one of them at least. The well which was dedicated to his mother St Non is only a mile/1.6km, if that, along a peaceful lane towards the sea. There are the ruins of a 14th century chapel in a field on the right and the well is situated on the left hand side of the path leading to them, with a statue of the Virgin Mary nearby on the other side. It is said that the well came into being immediately the saint was born, around 462 A.D. in the middle of a thunder storm, and that his mother left with him for Brittany shortly afterwards. By the mid-1700s, the well's arched stone roof had been restored by Dr John Davies, the Chantor of St David's Cathedral.

The healing properties were general, with pins and coins being dropped in it, but children merely 'dipped' in. In the early 18th century, Browne Willis wrote:

'There is a fine Well beside it (St Non's chapel), covered with a stone roof, and inclos'd within a Wall, with Benches to sit upon round the Well. Some old simple People go still to visit this Saint at some particular times, expecially upon St Non's Day (March 2) which they keep holy, and offer Pins, Pebbles, Etc. at this well.'

These days, there are obviously still some 'old and simple people' (and some not so old and simple) about for there is still the odd coin thrown in here. In late summer, large quantities of hydrangea blossoms that are blown in by the wind give it a mystic quality.

St Non's well has seen centuries of pilgrimages. One specially recorded event occurred in 1951 following restoration and rededication.

As has been said, the old chapel is a ruin, having been demolished in 1810, but a new one was built in 1934. This stands on the coastal side of St Non's Retreat with its splendid view across the water, and it is well worth a visit. The holy water stoup inside on the left came from Capel y Gwrhyd, another ancient chapel reduced to a few stones some little distance away near Rhodiad y Brenin.

St Justinians

Two or three miles west of Tyddewi/St David's is another holy well near St Justinian's chape,l situated on the coast overlooking Ynys Dewi (Ramsey Island). Its waters were well known for their healing qualities. Francis Jones (2) records that 'A man suffering from a swelling in his stomach, drank from it, became very sick, then threw up a frog, and was cured immediately!' Possibly the frog was not already in his stomach, but went down with the water with predictable results.

One of the stories of St Justinian belongs to the 'severed head' variety often associated with saints. He was a Breton – small in stature and a friend and confessor to St David. Being strict in his ways, he became somewhat disenchanted with the way the monastery was run and decided to isolate himself from the constant stream of devotees. This he did by attacking the causeway with an axe, each blow breaking off pieces to form menacing tidal rocks – now known as the Bitches and the Axe – until he finally separated Ynys Dewi from the mainland. This unsociable behaviour did not go down very well with his followers who in turn took an axe to him and cut off his head. Thereupon, the saint, undeterred, returned to the mainland with, as the old song says 'his head tucked underneath his arm' and set it down on the cliff top. Immediately a spring gushed up. The redoubtable little Breton was then buried nearby at the chapel site.

Ynys Dewi/Ramsey Island is reached by boat from St Justinians from April to September, usually a journey of about a quarter of an hour, depending upon the weather. You can stay overnight in a farmhouse. Alternatively, there are boat trips right around the island from which you may view lots of Atlantic Grey seals.

Llanllawer

Take the B4318 out of Abergwaun (Fishguard) for about two and a half miles (3.5km) and turn left for Llanllawer, continue for approximately half a mile (800m), crossing Afon Gwaun and ignoring the turn to the right. You will then negotiate a couple of sharp bends before coming to the little well of Llanllawer on the left in a field near the church. Once thought to be also called Ffynnon Gapan, It has an arched roof constructed from rough masonry.

Many used to immerse themselves in Ffynnon Llanllawer at one time. Its healing properties were various but it was especially beneficial for eye conditions. It was also a 'pin' well which if tossed in bent served for a curse and if straight indicated goodwill. Coins were also used and, as with many still existing wells, present day visitors have been known to throw one in for luck. Isolated Llanllawer has Neolithic Cromlechs and Standing Stones nearby and is beautifully situated with a fine view over Trecwm gorge to the southwest.

Trefin (between Tyddewi (St David's) and Abergwaun (Fishguard) equidistant to both)
It is quite fitting to use Trefin to illustrate the typical village well, this being the place where the late Francis Jones whose comprehensive book *The Holy Wells of Wales* is much quoted – was born in 1908.

There are several springs which at one time served the community regularly, and still do when it freezes hard – which in this corner of Wales, is not often. A small one, which has been nicely preserved with a little blue painted door left open, is to be seen on the left hand side of the hill down to the cove of Aber Felin. At the top of the village, the pump has been recently restored and dispenses drinking water to any who care to use it. It is helpful if the pump is used regularly – and the local children cannot believe their luck. The well that feeds it is six feet (2.4m) wide and is twenty feet (6m) down. It was originally 'hand dug' by one man and a boy and unlike most wells it is not ringed, the rock being sufficiently solid to make this unnecessary.

MAESYFED (RADNORSHIRE)

'Comfortable bath chairs, with reliable men in charge, are an indispensable acquisition to a health resort.' W.J. Bufton 1894

Ffynnon Dewi, Llanfadarn Fynydd, situated at Llaethdy, three miles (5km) west of Llanbadarn Fynydd (A483) between Llandrindod and Newtown)
This was once very popular, attracting people from afar to seek cures from its water, which had a small sulphur content, the properties of which were said to have been discovered by a local blacksmith. The spring was piped downhill from a nearby field into a stone trough which was 3' (1.2m) wide by about 3_' (1.35,) in depth, and that overflowed into the Llaethdy stream a few yards to the north.

People frequently bathed their dogs in this water, its sulphur content being a good cure for mange. One George Augustus Haigh of Penithon Hall regularly came along to give his canine friends a wash here.

In the 19th century there would have been a considerable number of people at Ffynnon Dewi on Sunday evenings and the area around it became known as St David's. These days, though the water is still clear, the well itself is overgrown with plant life.

Blaen Edw Wells, Llandeglau, (Llandeglau is situated about five miles /8km north-east of Llandrindod Wells on the A44, which was once the old stage coach route to the latter).
Now no more than a stinking ditch, this watering place was once very well known. It was mentioned in the *Cambrian Balnea* in 1825 as 'a very strong sulphurous spring opposite the inn' and a 19th century guide book states that 'this vitriolic water' was said to cure 'St Tegla's' (or 'falling') disease. (Whether this ailment arose from too much indulgence at the inn is not stated.) Cooke's *Typography* (1830) describes the water as 'covered with brown scum . . . an abominable stench . . . but not unpleasant taste'. It is remarkable how, in times past, people would sample anything which was so unpalatable. But that they habitually did so is evident by the many

accounts of the appearance and smell of springs, especially the sulphurous ones. Perhaps one should bear in mind that it is the 'discoveries' of cures that were recorded rather than the number of trusting souls who expired from the results of such experiments.

There was also a chalybeate spring beside a nearby brook and the iron content of this is recorded as being very high. Indeed, it was nearly five times as strong as that at Trefriw in north Wales.

Presumably, many visitors stayed at Llandrindod for there is little accommodation here. One 19th century writer commented on the 'scarcity of lodgings' and stated that 'the uninviting character of the surrounding scenery retarded their (wells) progress'. This was a very undeserved slur.

Buildings were erected and a bath was available at the spring but, by the 1930's, the place became derelict and the good people of the little village of Llandeglau were left in peace.

Llandrindod Wells

'Men come from far, sad, hopeless pilgrims,
to the font of health,
Groaning on crutches, but depart without;
Seized wild the vessels, drank and were made whole,
And all did bless Llandrindod' (1906 Guide Book)

Unlike the other mid-Wales Spas, Llandrindod, architecturally, was 'custom built'. The unsuspecting traveller, pottering peacefully along surrounded by hills, sheep and farmhouses, suddenly finds him or herself confronted with immense red brick terrace buildings. This is because, as a town at least, it did not exist before the 'heyday' of the waters and the arrival of the railway line (which, thankfully, is still running). That is not to say that the waters weren't there – they were just not famous. The Romans, who had large forts here (the remains of one are known as Castell Collen, about a mile [1.6km] north west of the town) had, as one might expect, availed themselves of the various springs, which they called Balnea Siluria. However, centuries were then to pass before the wells themselves became a thriving industry. There are records of local use in the 17th century of one of the saline springs.

In 1736, a Mrs Jenkins came across both a sulphur and saline spring and in 1748 a contributor to the 'Gentleman's Magazine' waxed more than lyrical – a couple of lines will suffice as his enthusiasm tends to overeach itself.

'Let England boast Bath's crowded springs
Llandrindod happier, Cambria sings.

Later, in 1756, Dr Wessel Linden published a paper upon the efficacy of Llandrindod water. Thus its reputation began to spread but, apart from needing a cure, the visitors at that time must have been pretty tough. Firstly, there was no proper road to Llandrindod, and the apology for one that was built in 1775 to connect up with the bumpy stretch that is now the A44, was uncomfortable in the extreme. Secondly, there was hardly anywhere to stay when you actually got there.

However, one enterprising gentleman, a Mr Grosvenor from Shrewsbury not only extended the few farmhouses but also, in 1749, upon a hill that overlooked a bog (that was later to become a man made boating lake) built a hotel that was large enough to accommodate many hundreds. It offered facilities that must have gladdened the hearts of the guests after their arduous journey. Whatever society required, they got – shops, hairdressing salons, billiards, racing, assemblies – all on site. There were however people who criticised its 'libertine' goings on. It appears that the locals also complained of damage to their farmland by the hunting fraternity. Whatever the reason, the lease was not renewed and by 1788, the hotel was no more. It was, however, still remembered decades later, which might indicate the kind of reputation it must have generated in its short existence. *Pryse's Handbook* of 1870 retrospectively praised its management but Lewis's *Topographical Dictionary* of 1833 did not.

After this little flurry of activity, Llandrindod, like the other Welsh spas, had to wait until the mid 19th century, by which time the railway had arrived and more springs had been discovered in two main locations. At the top of the town, there were Mrs Jenkins' sulphur and saline springs along with the grand Pump House

Hotel, which had two tarrifs for first and second class visitors in grand Victorian style. In the centre, tremendous development took place with five storey buildings for apartments and guest houses and down below in the pleasant shelter of the woodland was the Rock Park Spa complete with Pump Room, treatment centre, music ensemble and hotel, and the High Street Baths above.

The springs had charming names 'Ffynnon Cwm-y-gof' and 'Ffynnon Llwyn-y-gog' after which the town was originally named.

In the late 19th century, charges for saline and sulphur waters were the same at both sites – three shillings and ninepence for a two gallon (9ltr) jar (one shilling and ninepence being refundable on the jar). A weekly ticket would cost you two shillings and sixpence and an early morning glass would be sixpence. For the rest of the day it was offered at a bargain price of one penny. It is important to remember that the waters were most beneficial when taken early in the morning. The chalybeate spring was free.

Ask any older resident how many visitors came here in the heyday of the spa, and the figure of 80,000 a year will roll off the tongue, together with the fact that the queues for the waters could be as much as two miles (3.2km) long. The thousands came for cures, which included many other things besides drinking several pints of water every day.

Part of the Rock Park Pump Room, which was built around 1867, consisted of a row of cubicles in which were housed some dire looking equipment that seemed more fit for a torture chamber. Behind this was a row of toilets – which says it all. Alas, although the Pump Room was saved and restored (and only just – for in the 1970's, it was so derelict that it was nearly pulled down), the rest was turned into a visitor centre and later a venue for health consultants. The cubicles were demolished as were the toilets. One cannot help but feel that those original artefacts would have been much more interesting to the modern visitor than a few mounted display boards and the couple of large baths that replaced them.

Among the famous visitors were Lloyd George and Prince Edward (before he became King Edward VIII/Duke of Windsor). There are many photographs of the latter in the various guide

Tariff of Baths, Treatments and Waters.

	s.	d.		s.	d.
Needle Spray (per 10 mins) (Plain or Sulphur) ...	3	3	Electrical or Vibratory Massage : 10 mins.	4	0
Course of six	18	0	20 ,,	5	0
Liver Pack and Needle Spray	5	0	30 ,,	6	0
Aix Douche and Massage	6	0	Cataphoresis (Ionic medication) per 20 mins.		
Vichy Douche and Massage ...	6	0	One Joint	6	6
Scotch Douche (per 10 min)	4	0	Two Joints	8	6
Electric Light or Radiant Heat Bath followed by Reclining Bath or Spray	7	0	Cataphoresis (preceded by other treatment)		
Dry Massage at Baths :			One Joint	4	6
,, 10 mins.	2	6	Two Joints	6	6
15 mins. 3 0 20 mins.	4	0	Cautery Treatment per application	3	0
30 mins. 5 0 40 mins	7	6	Bergonie Obesity Treatment, 20/30 mins, ...	8	0
Leucodescent Treatment :			30/45 ,, ...	10	0
10 mins.	3	0	45/60 ,, ...	13	0
20 ,, ...	6	0	Schnee Four Cell Bath. 20 mins.	6	0
Tyrnauer Electrical Hot Air Treatment :			Schnee Two Cell Bath. 20 mins.	4	6
One Limb or Spine	6	0	Reclining Sulphur Bath (per 10 mins.)	3	3
Two Limbs	8	0	Ditto course of six	18	0
Whole Body	7	0	Sulphur Reclining or Needle Spray with Douche	4	0
Local Peat Pack (single)	5	0	Ditto, course of six	23	0
(double)	6	0	Whirlpool Bath (Hands or Feet)	5	0
Massage following another Treatment : 10 mins.	2	0	Ditto, with Peat	6	0
15 mins. 2 6 20 mins.	3	0	Diathermy or Thermo Penetration, 20 mins.	7	0
30 mins. 4 0 40 mins.	6	0	30 mins. 10/- 40 mins.	12	6
Plombieres and Tivoli Treatment	7	6	Sunlight Treatment up to 10 mins. 4/-, 15 mins. 5/-. 20 mins. 6/-, 30 mins.	7	0
Plombieres Treatment without Tivoli	6	0	Vita Heat Light Treatment with Massage 20 mins.	5	0
Nauheim Baths	6	0	without ,, ..	2	6
X Ray Radiograph from	10	6			
X Ray Exam. or T'ment	6	6			
Effervescing Pine Bath	6	0			
Galvanic, Faradic or Bristow Coil Current :					
5 mins. 2/-, 10 mins. 4/-, 20 mins	5	6			

MEDICINAL WATERS – Radium Sulphur, Lithia Saline, Magnesium, and Chalybeate.
1d per Glass. Day Ticket 6d. (limiting holder to 8 glasses).
Supplying Jar of Water and delivering same to Local Hotels and Boarding Houses before 9 a.m., 5/- per week, or 9d. per morning per person.

books, dressed in a boy scouts uniform and drinking the water. Everyone was delighted when he said 'Your spa is in a lovely setting' but his comments on the taste of the potion do not seem to have been recorded!

During the Second World War, although taking the waters was beginning to be less fashionable, one could still obtain them at the Rock Park Pump Room, listen to a musical ensemble and even attend tea dances. The latter were much favoured by members of the Officers Training Corps who were stationed in the town – much to the enjoyment of the local girls whom they outnumbered by about fifty to one.

In this beautiful spot the chalybeate spring still trickles away near the Arlais Brook, a few yards from the Pump Room. This 'Rock Spout' was given, as the inscription above it says, 'for the use of the public by the Lord of the Manor, J.W. Gibson Watt Esq. 1879'. It is said that local authorities made attempts to make a charge for the chalybeate water but that every time they implemented this, the water stopped running.

The nearest Llandrindod water, not being sacred, can come to the mysterious is the story of a Mr Pilot, employed to put up tents for a forthcoming auction, who dreamed about the existence of a saline spring in the Rock Park. The next day he went to look and found it in the exact place where it had appeared in his dream. The tale becomes more and more believable because it keeps getting passed on from book to book – and here it is again! However, the gentleman did exist. In the 1980's, someone who visited the local tourist office happened to mention that she was a descendant, now living some thirty miles (48km) away in Newtown.

The eye well issues at varying degrees of strength from the same rock as the chalybeate spring. It is somewhat lower down, and the water seeps straight into the Arlais Brook. It is now reduced in appearance to a muddy puddle that is often clogged with leaves, but the 'Friends of the Rock Park' hope to restore it. At one time it was regularly used and, in the old days, there was an established ritual attendant upon it. A set number of paces had to be taken whilst muttering an incantation as one approached the well and upon arrival, the right hand was dipped into the water so as to bathe the right eye, following the same procedure with the left. If the eyes tingled and ran, it was a good sign – provided that the sufferer did not wipe them.

There were numerous 'discoveries' of bogus chalybeate springs when drinking the waters was popular. Anything rust coloured was lighted upon with enthusiasm and a 19th century guide book records that even mud was once sent away for analysis. This is not as crazy as it sounds. The iron content is invaluable but the water certainly does turn brown after a while. In the 1980's, the manager of Llandrindod's largest hotel, entertaining a group of journalists, thought it would be a good idea to give them all a small glass of chalybeate water before their dinner. The spout trickles very slowly and it was the task of the local tourist officer to stand patiently by the spring filling containers for the exercise. Unfortunately, she did this in the morning and by evening, the water had turned a singularly unappetising looking rust colour. The hotelier, never short of ideas, poured a little bicarbonate of soda and some salt into tap water, and as this tasted strange enough to be believable, it was a great success. Some of the party, obviously martyrs to indigestion, even declared that their meal had gone down 'very well' after it.

Rock Park offered saline, chalybeate, magnesium and sulphur and, up until a few years ago, you could try them all. Then, some inexplicable EEC regulation questioned the latter two and the ruling is still to be resolved. Meanwhile, the pumps remain over the marble counter awaiting their fate. One cannot help wondering why they should find a problem with something which people had been downing by the pint over several centuries.

Any disappointment at being unable to sample the sulphur might easily be allayed by consideration of G.A. Cook's (3) comments in the 1830s, which point out that it is a 'purgatory of no mean order' adding that 'when thrown on hot iron, it emits a blue flame and smells like brimstone'. This is not an exaggeration for it smelled bad enough in the glass. His other useful information is that it changes silver leaves to gold in six minutes, and is best used for an artificial bath. Was this a 19th century equivalent of self tanning lotion! It was best to drink the saline water between March and November but it was more beneficial if you were 'bled' before doing so.

There will, hopefully, soon be plenty of saline water available again free of charge in the Pump Room (they are at present waiting upon the local council regarding access for cleaning of filters). Meanwhile you can visit the salad bar, partake of a hot meal, a snack and even alcoholic beverages. It is open seven days a week from 9.30 a.m. until 6.30 p.m. (Friday & Saturday 10 p.m.) There is a feasibility study in progress with a view to possibly enhancing the facilities. The ultimate aim is a Hydrotherapy Centre but about three million pounds of private investment is needed and those concerned may have to settle for something a little less ambitious.

The magnificent Pump House Hotel at the top of the town and its counterpart in Rock Park are long gone. The latter is even threatened with some new housing development. The former was rebuilt in 1888 and survived in its grandeur for some time, before serving as a convalescent home, a teacher's training college and a school. It was finally occupied by Powys County Council who managed to overload it to such an extent with filing cabinets full of paper that its structure became unsound. Discussion took place about demolishing it, the proposal was voted through, yet another piece of paper was filed within, and the collapse was complete – before most of the local population realised it. In its place arose the bog standard pagoda type council building. All that remains of the hotel is the boiler house, now full of high technology for use at meetings.

Ffynnon Fair, Pyllylai/Pilleth (about five miles from Trefyclo/Knighton on the B4356)
The well is situated in the churchyard, to the north of the tower, and was thought to be beneficial for eye diseases.

After the battle of Pilleth in 1402, the victorious survivors of Owain Glyndwr's army were said to have refreshed themselves at Ffynnon Fair.

The well is oblong in shape and restoration in 1910 revealed steps down to it. Unfortunately, access these days is impeded by a piece of wood but visitors can still quench their thirst by using the cup that dangles on a string over the well.

BIBLIOGRAPHY

T.R. Roberts: *The Spas of Wales*, John Hoggs, London 1897 (1)
Francis Jones: *The Holy Wells of Wales*, University Press, Cardiff 1992 (2)
G.A. Cooke: *Topographical and Statistical Description of the Principality of Wales*, London 1830 (3)
Fred J. Hando: *Here and there in Monmouthshire* (4)
Also
Ancient and Historical Monuments in Wales – Caernarfonshire, Carmarthenshire (Vol. II), Meirionnydd, Pembrokeshire
Graham Adamson: *Ffynnon Fair and Dôl Belidr*, 1979
W.J. Bufton: *The Rambler Guide to Llandrindod Wells*, F. Hodgson, London 1906
Denbighshire County Council: *Enjoy Medieval Denbighshire*
W.B. Jones and E.A. Freeman: *The History and Antiquities of St David*, Pembs, 1856
W.J. Lewis: *Born on a Perilous Rock*, Cambrian News 1980
Ordnance Survey: *Leisure Guide Brecon Beacons and Mid Wales*, Automobile Assoc. 1989
Menna Owen: *Cefn's Historic Holy Well*, 1977
T.J.L. Prichard: *Aberystwyth Guide*, 1824
Nona Rees: *St David of Dewisland*, Gomer Press, Llandysul 1997
John Rhys M.A. Ll.D.: *Sacred Wells of Wales*
Alan Roderick: *Folklore of Gwent*, Village Publishing, Cwmbran 1983 (5)
F.M. Slater and C. Saxon: *Mid Wales Spas and Mineral Springs*, Powys County Council 1982
Transactions of the Honourable Society of Cymmrodorion Sessions 1892-93
Trelech – A Brief History of the Town, The Trelech Society
A.W. Wade-Evans: *Life of St David*, London 1923
A.W. Wade-Evans: *Vitae Sanctorum Britanniae et Genealogiae*, Cardiff 1944
John Ward: *Our Lady of Pen-rhys*, Archaeologia Cambrensis, July 1914
Wellsprings Fellowship: *Eluned's Way*, Brecon 1999
Will O'Whispers: *A Chalybeate Well gimmick*, Cambrian News, April 1976

ACKNOWLEDGEMENTS

Eirlys Gruffydd, Welsh Wells Society
Judith Hurford
Monmouth Archaeological Society
Melanie Price